DUAL LANGUAGE

La primera vez

Me corto el cabello

Melinda Radabaugh
Traducción de Patricia Cano

Heinemann Library
Chicago, Illinois

©2003 Heinemann Library
a division of Reed Elsevier Inc.
Chicago, Illinois

Customer Service   888-454-2279
Visit our website at www.heinemannlibrary.com

Designed by Sue Emerson, Heinemann Library
Printed and bound in the United States by Lake Book Manufacturing, Inc.

07 06 05 04 03
10 9 8 7 6 5 4 3 2 1

Library of Congress Cataloging-in-Publication Data
Radabaugh, Melinda Beth.
   [Getting a haircut. Spanish]
   Me corto el cabello / Melinda Radabaugh; traducción de Patricia Cano.
      p.cm. -- (La primera vez)
   Includes index.
   Translated from the English.
   Summary: Describes what to expect on your first visit to the barber shop or salon for a haircut, discussing the big chair, smocks, shampoo, haircutting tools, and blow-dryer.
   ISBN 1-4034-0233-7 (HC), 1-4034-0471-2 (Pbk.)
1. Haircutting--Juvenile literature. [1. Haircutting. 2. Spanish language materials.] I. Title. II. Series.
   TT970 .R3318 2002
   646. 7'24--dc21

                                    2002032706

Acknowledgments
The author and publishers are grateful to the following for permission to reproduce copyright material:
p. 4 Norbert Schafer/Corbis; p. 5L George Shelley/Corbis; p. 5R Bob Krist/Corbis; p. 6 Charles Gupton/Corbis; p. 7L Robert Lifson/Heinemann Library; p. 7R Eyewire Collection/Getty Images; pp. 8, 9, 12, 13, 16, 18, 19T, 20, 21, 24T Greg Williams/Heinemann Library; p. 10 Linda Phillips/PhotoResearchers; p. 11 Evan Kafka/Liaison/Getty Images; p. 14 Jack Ballard/Visuals Unlimited; p. 15 Summer Productions; p. 17 Amor Montes De Oca; p. 19B Roger Ressmeyer/Corbis; p. 22 (row 1, L–R) Greg Williams/Heinemann Library, PhotoDisc; p. 22 (row 2, L–R) John A. Rizzo/Getty Images, PhotoDisc; p. 22 (row 3, L–R) Greg Williams/Heinemann Library, RDF/Visuals Unlimited; p. 23 (row 1) Greg Williams/Heinemann Library; p. 23 (row 2, L–R) Eyewire Collection/Getty Images, Greg Williams/Heinemann Library, Greg Williams/Heinemann Library; p. 23 (row 3, L–R) PhotoDisc, Bob Krist/Corbis, Jack Ballard/Visuals Unlimited; p. 24 (top, L–R) Greg Williams/Heinemann Library, PhotoDisc; p. 24B PhotoDisc; back cover (L–R) PhotoDisc, Greg Williams/Heinemann Library

Cover photograph by Greg Williams/Heinemann Library
Photo research by Amor Montes de Oca

Every effort has been made to contact copyright holders of any material reproduced in this book. Any omissions will be rectified in subsequent printings if notice is given to the publisher.

Special thanks to our bilingual advisory panel for their help in the preparation of this book:

Anita R. Constantino
Literacy Specialist
Irving Independent School District
Irving, TX

Aurora Colón García
Literacy Specialist
Northside Independent School District
San Antonio, TX

Argentina Palacios
Docent
Bronx Zoo
New York, NY

Leah Radinsky
Bilingual Teacher
Inter-American Magnet School
Chicago, IL

Ursula Sexton
Researcher, WestEd
San Ramon, CA

Special thanks to the Vance and Opp families for their assistance with the photographs in this book.

Unas palabras están en negrita, **así**.
Las encontrarás en el glosario en fotos de la página 23.

Contenido

¿Por qué nos cortamos el cabello?

A algunas personas les gusta
el cabello corto.

Se lo cortan cuando está largo.

A veces queremos otro **peinado**.

Un corte de cabello cambia
el peinado.

¿Dónde nos cortan el cabello?

A unos niños les cortan el cabello en la casa.

Se lo corta un adulto.

Unos niños van a una **peluquería.**

Otros van a una **barbería.**

¿Qué es una barbería?

Una **barbería** es un lugar donde cortan el cabello.

Adentro tiene sillas y grandes espejos.

Los **barberos** cortan el cabello.

¿Qué es una peluquería?

Una **peluquería** es un lugar donde hacen **peinados**.

También cortan el cabello.

Adentro tiene sillas y grandes espejos.

Los **peluqueros** cortan el cabello.

¿Qué pasa en la barbería?

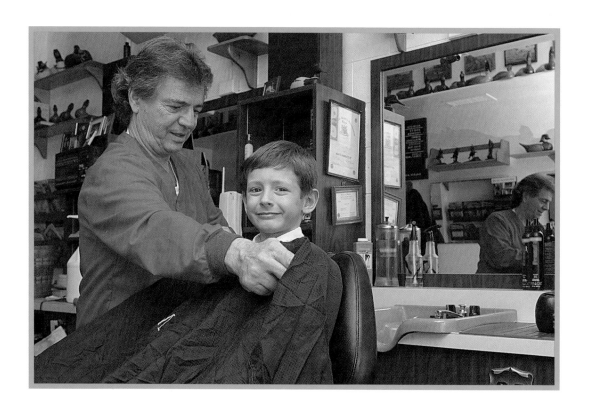

Nos sentamos en una silla alta.

El **barbero** nos pone una **capa**.

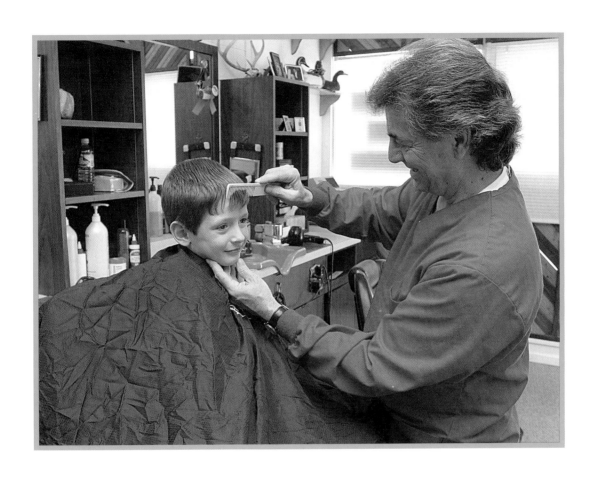

Así no nos cae el cabello en la ropa.

El barbero nos pasa el peine.

¿Qué pasa en la peluquería?

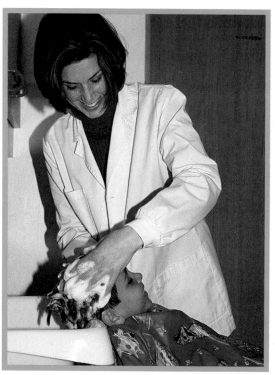 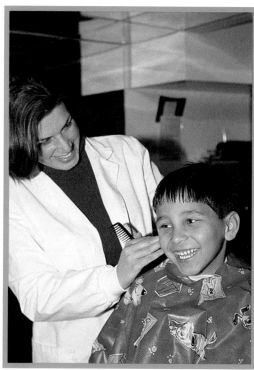

El **peluquero** nos lava la cabeza.

Después nos sentamos en la silla de peluquería.

El **peluquero** nos corta el cabello.

Después lo seca con un **secador**.

¿Con qué nos cortan el cabello?

Los **barberos** y los **peluqueros**
cortan el cabello con **tijeras**.

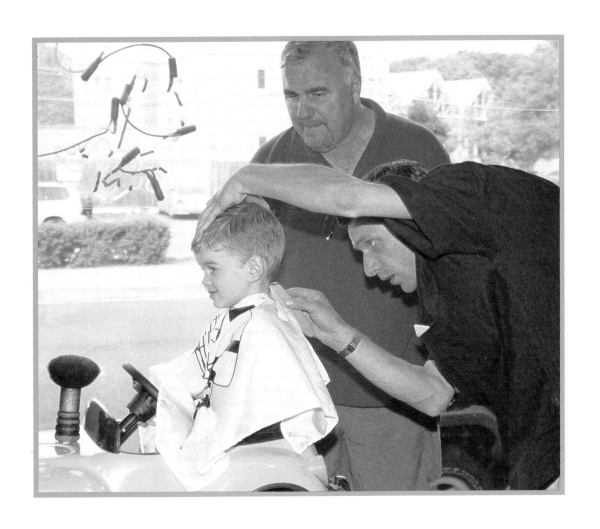

A veces usan una **maquinilla**.

¿Qué se siente?

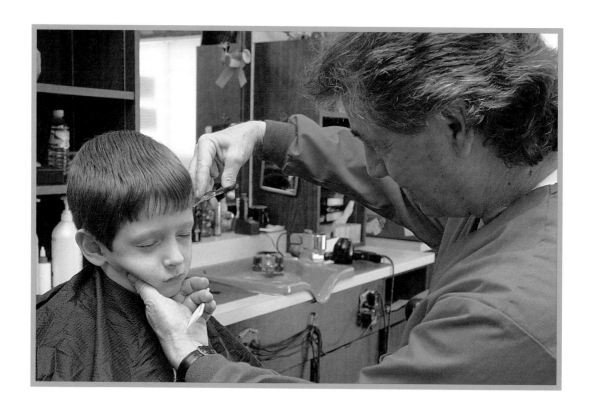

Un corte de cabello no duele.

Pero tenemos que estar
muy quietos.

La **maquinilla** zumba y nos hace cosquillas.

El aire del **secador** es caliente.

¿Qué pasa después?

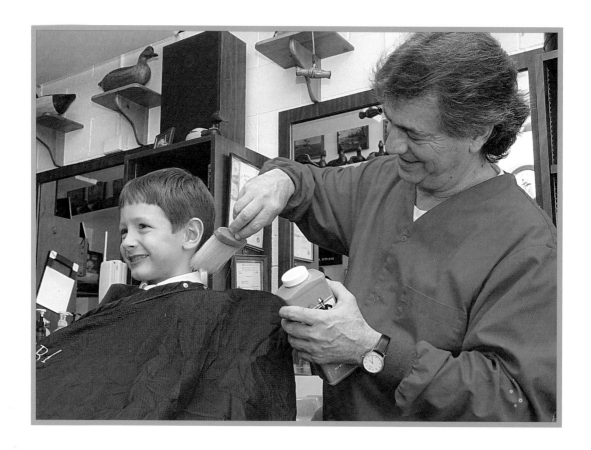

El **barbero** o el **peluquero** nos quita los pelitos con un cepillo.

Nos quita la **capa**.

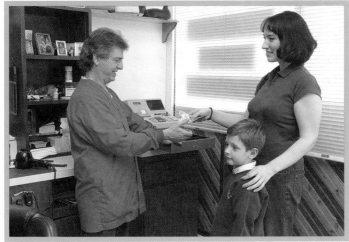

Miramos en un espejo cómo quedamos.

Pagamos por el corte y nos vamos.

Prueba

¿Qué vemos en una **barbería** o en una **peluquería?**

Busca las respuestas en la página 24.

 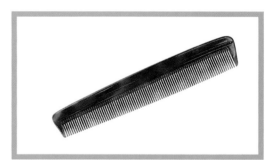

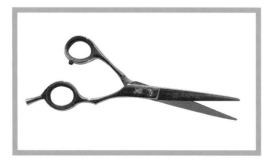 

Glosario en fotos

barbero
páginas 9, 12, 13, 16, 20

capa
páginas 12, 13, 20

peluquería
páginas 7, 10–11, 14, 22

barbería
páginas 7, 8–9, 12, 22

maquinilla
páginas 17, 19

tijeras
página 16

secador
páginas 15, 19

peinado
páginas 5, 10

peluquera
páginas 11, 14, 15, 16, 20

Nota a padres y maestros

Leer para buscar información es un aspecto importante del desarrollo de la lectoescritura. El aprendizaje empieza con una pregunta. Si usted alienta a los niños a hacerse preguntas sobre el mundo que los rodea, los ayudará a verse como investigadores. Cada capítulo de este libro empieza con una pregunta. Lean la pregunta juntos, miren las fotos y traten de contestar la pregunta. Después, lean y comprueben si sus predicciones son correctas. Piensen en otras preguntas sobre el tema y comenten dónde pueden buscar la respuesta. Ayude a los niños a usar el glosario en fotos y el índice para practicar nuevas destrezas de vocabulario y de investigación.

Índice

Respuestas de la página 22

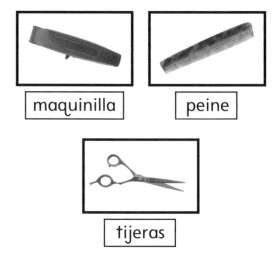

maquinilla

peine

tijeras

24

Kata Golda's Hand-Stitched Felt

Kata Golda's
Hand-Stitched Felt

25 Whimsical Sewing Projects

KATA GOLDA

photographs by FRANK WHITE

STC CRAFT | A MELANIE FALICK BOOK

STEWART, TABORI & CHANG · NEW YORK

Published in 2009 by Stewart, Tabori & Chang
An imprint of Harry N. Abrams, Inc.

Text and illustrations copyright © 2009 by Kata Golda
Photographs copyright © 2009 by Frank White

Library of Congress Cataloging-in-Publication Data
Golda, Kata.
[Hand-stitched felt]
Kata Golda's hand-stitched felt : 25 whimsical sewing projects / by Kata Golda ; photography by Frank White.
p. cm.
ISBN 978-1-58479-798-2
1. Needlework. 2. Fancy work. 3. Felt. I. Title. II. Title:
Hand-stitched felt.
TT750.G626 2009
746'.0463--dc22   2008050580

Editor **Liana Allday**
Designer **woolypear**
Production Manager **Jacqueline Poirier**

The text of this book was composed in Kievit.

Printed and bound in China
10 9 8 7 6 5 4 3 2 1

HNA
harry n. abrams, inc.
a subsidiary of La Martinière Groupe

115 West 18th Street
New York, NY 10011
www.hnabooks.com

To Joy, my greatest mentor

Contents

Introduction

I have been surrounded by stitchers my entire life, and they have been my greatest sources of inspiration. As a child, I remember my grandmother Sylvia knitting fancy sweaters on tiny needles, crocheting colorful afghans, and cross-stitching intricate Norman Rockwell paintings. My mother, Joy, filled my life with color and domesticity, always doing handwork or cooking up elegantly simple, tasty meals. I still marvel when I recall the way she would arrange her irregularly chopped beets, parsnips, carrots, and rutabaga around a plate of sautéed green beans. I loved accompanying her to her knitting and needlepoint shop in St. Paul, Minnesota, where I spent hours hanging hanks of needlepoint yarn on big hooks that covered an entire wall, organizing them by their subtle gradations of color. I think about this now when I stack felt on the shelves in my studio, realizing that I learned more about color from my mother and her yarn shop than I did in art theory class in college.

I have studied many types of art and worked in a variety of artistic fields, from photography and sculpture to bookbinding and quilting, but the craft materials of my childhood—thread, fabric, yarn, and paper—have informed my best work. I had spent some time working as a professional quilter by the time I had my baby girl, Odette, in 1999. I wanted to stitch soft things for her, but I found that what I was dreaming up for Odette was very different than the commissioned quilts I was piecing together and hand-quilting. Instead of using cotton I chose to sew mostly with wool felt, which came in an incredible range of colors and was wonderful to touch. Plus, I was enchanted by the fact that felt would not unravel, so I could simply leave the clean, cut edges unhemmed and complete a project in almost no time at all. Instead of the straight, small, and precise stitches I was required to produce for my quilts, I chose to sew larger, more irregular stitches in contrasting thread colors. I fancied the way the "imperfections" in my stitches showed the presence of my hand in the work. I sewed everything from stuffed animals and balls to pillows and finger puppets, and when Odette was old enough to hold a crayon, I bound a drawing book for her, its covers made from felt-covered boards adorned with an appliquéd bear and her name. Though I did not know it at the time, this was the beginning of my business—Kata Golda—which now includes many of the handmade creations in this book, which are sold in nearly a hundred shops across the country, and even in places as far away as Japan and Brazil.

What I love to do is always shifting, but the central question has remained the same: Am I loving the way I spend each day? Running a business, raising a child, and trying to keep a house orderly are not always easy, and require discipline, prioritizing, and love. I always feel especially lucky when I have finished folding a stack of freshly laundered towels and am reminded of the stacks of felt awaiting me in my studio. Suddenly, my mind is free of household obligations, my daughter is off at school, and I am able to delve into my creative work with excitement and focus. I step into my studio, open my tool pocket, which is packed with exactly what I need, and begin stitching. With this book, I hope that you, too, will be inspired to create your own large, colorful, and uniquely imperfect stitches.

PART 1

Sewing Techniques

Tools and Materials

Basic Tool List

Fabric shears

Small scissors

Paper scissors

Straight pins

Hand-sewing needles

Safety pins

Pencil

Fine-tipped permanent marker

Glue stick

1" x 12" transparent ruler

6" x 24" transparent ruler

Tape measure

Self-healing cutting mat

Rotary cutter (great for cutting out large pieces of felt with straight edges)

Before you get started on the projects in this book, make sure that you have on hand the basic materials and tools listed here. Additional supplies and specific felt and embroidery floss recommendations are called for in the materials list at the beginning of each project.

Wool Felt

I prefer to work with pure wool felt or felt that is about 70 percent wool and 30 percent rayon. Wool has an extraordinary natural beauty, a matte finish that is soft to the touch, and an elastic quality that works well with large stitches. It is also water-resistant, flame-resistant, and warm. Though synthetic felt fabrics can work in a pinch, they tend to look shiny and feel a bit plasticky.

At Kata Golda we dye our own felt with everything from plants to Kool-Aid. To find out about buying our felt and other wool felt, check the Resources on page 126.

Sewing with Wool Felt

Here are some important points to keep in mind when sewing with wool felt:

- *Wool felt is incredibly strong and durable and can be used in projects that may experience strain over time.*

- *Wool felt is made from compressed animal fibers that interlock and become uniformly matted, so the cut edges can be left raw and will not unravel. This makes for extra quick sewing projects, since there is no need to hem or finish edges.*

- *Both sides of wool felt look the same, so the side on which you stitch the design will become the "right side," and the side on which you tie your knots will become the back or "wrong side."*

- *Projects made from wool felt are perfect for beginning sewers since, if you make a mistake and need to pull out your stitches, the marks won't show in the fabric.*

- *Over time, wool felt may stretch. If it does, trim off the excess and restitch the seam for a snugger fit.*

CLEANING WOOL FELT

Pure wool felt and high-wool-content felt will shrink when washed in warm or hot water. I recommend hand-washing wool felt in cold water with mild detergent. To dry the felt, lay it on a towel and roll it up, gently twisting the ends of the towel to wring out the excess water. Then lay the felt on a dry towel and reshape it, if necessary. You can simply line-dry small items once you have removed excess water. To remove a stubborn stain, blot the stain with warm water, but do not scrub or you may cause discoloration and distortion.

FELT SCRAPS

When I sew I accumulate a huge quantity of scraps. Rather than throwing them out, I hang on to them in order to create patchwork (see page 17), appliqués, or small projects such as the Finger Puppets on page 74. I like to organize my scraps by color and size so that they are readily available when I am creating new designs.

Embroidery Floss

Each of the projects in this book is sewn with embroidery floss, which is available in a wide variety of colors and can be found inexpensively at most craft and fabric stores. Embroidery floss is made up of six plies (or strands) of cotton thread that are twisted together. You can use the embroidery floss as you purchased it (with all six strands), or you can separate the plies to create thinner floss. In each project I recommend the number of plies that should be used, depending on the purpose of the stitches as well as what I think will look best. For instance, if my stitches need to be extra strong, such as those used to attach loops to the Patchwork Curtain on page 96, I might use six plies of floss. But for more delicate stitches, like those used to appliqué the letters on Odette's Door Sign (see page 86), I might only use one ply of floss.

To separate the six-ply floss into the desired number of plies, cut off a length of floss (about 18"), then, starting near the center of the piece, gently pull apart the number of plies you need. Be sure to pull gently or you will create a knotty mess. Keep the remaining strands nice and neat so that you can use them later in the project or in future projects.

Separating plies of embroidery floss

Stitches and Knots

Basic Stitches

If the projects in this book look simple to make, that's because they are. Only a few basic stitches are used, and they are all worked by hand.

When it comes to stitches, I like to put more emphasis on individuality than consistency, though, as a general rule of thumb for the projects in this book, stitches should be roughly ⅛" to ¼" long and about the same distance apart, which is much larger than average hand-sewing stitches. We have four different hand-stitchers at Kata Golda, and I can tell the difference between each of their sewing styles at a glance—all different and all beautiful. I encourage you to experiment with your own stitching style, as well.

The projects in this book can be sewn with a wide variety of hand-sewing needles. I prefer #3 sharps because they are a bit longer, thicker, and sturdier than most needles, which is perfect for sewing felt, but other similar sizes will work.

STRAIGHT STITCH (OR RUNNING STITCH)

To sew a straight stitch, bring the needle up from the wrong side of the felt at the place where you would like to begin stitching. Bring the needle back through the felt, about ¼" from the point of entry. Continue in this manner to create a line of stitches spaced approximately ¼" apart. See drawing at left.

DOUBLE RUNNING STITCH

To create a double running stitch, first sew a line of straight stitches, as described above. Then go back and sew another line of straight stitches, filling in the empty spaces between the stitches in the first line. I often sew a double running stitch in two different colors to add visual interest. See drawing at left.

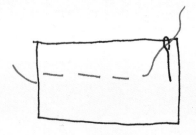

STRAIGHT (RUNNING) STITCH

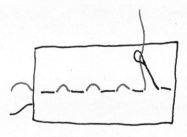

DOUBLE RUNNING STITCH

WHIPSTITCH EDGES

WHIPSTITCH APPLIQUÉ

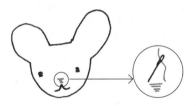

TRADITIONAL SATIN STITCH

RUSTIC SATIN STITCH

BLANKET STITCH

WHIPSTITCH

In this book, whipstitch is used either to join the edges of two pieces of felt or to attach an appliqué.

To join edges, knot off between the layers or on the back side, bring the needle up through the top fabric, then down around both edges, then push it through both layers of fabric. Keep working round and round the edge, keeping stitches ⅛" to ¼" apart, until the pieces are attached, then knot off between layers or on the backside. See drawing at left.

To attach an appliqué, knot off and insert the needle from the wrong side. Bring the needle up through the background felt, just outside the edge of the appliqué, and push back down through the right side about ⅛" inside the perimeter of the appliqué. Continue working the stitches approximately ⅛" to ¼" apart around the entire appliqué and knot off on the wrong side. See drawing at left.

SATIN STITCH

I use satin stitches to color in areas like noses and eyes. This can be done by sewing stitches, all going in one direction, to cover a given space entirely, being careful not to stitch "outside of the lines." To sew a satin stitch, knot off on the wrong side and bring the thread repeatedly from right side to wrong side, repeating the stitch in the same direction each time. When you can no longer see the fabric beneath the stitches, knot off on the wrong side. See drawing at left.

For a more rustic effect, a satin stitch can also be sewn with stitches going every which way. See drawing at left.

BLANKET STITCH

The blanket stitch can be used to finish the edge of a single-layer piece, like a blanket (hence its name), or to join the edges of two stacked pieces of felt. To sew a blanket stitch, knot off on the wrong side (or between the layers if sewing two pieces of felt), and bring the needle up to the right side of the work, ⅛" to ¼" from the edge. Bring the needle down around the edge and insert the needle again at the original point of entry (or in the bottom layer beneath the original point of entry, if sewing two pieces of felt). Catch the loop made from the first stitch with the working thread and insert the needle about ⅛" to ¼" away for next stitch. Repeat the process to continue stitching. See drawing at left.

FRENCH KNOT

DOUBLE KNOT

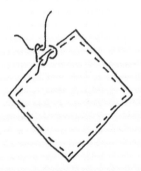

SQUARE KNOT

FRENCH KNOT

French knots can be decorative, or they can be used to appliqué pieces together. To tie a French knot, thread the needle with 6-ply floss and knot off on the wrong side of the work. Bring the needle through to the right side of the work and wrap the floss tightly around the needle, near the tip, three times. Hold the coil of thread in place with your finger or thumb while you bring the needle back through to the wrong side as close to the first stitch as possible without piercing it. Knot off on the wrong side to secure the knot. See drawing at left.

Basic Knots

As with most of my stitching, I like to keep knots simple when I sew. Most of the time I tie double knots at the end of my sewing strand, knotting one thread to itself twice. To do this, thread your needle and make two knots, one right on top of the other, at the end of your thread tail (see drawing at left). You can also make a double knot at the end of a line of stitches.

Other times, particularly if I am stitching around the perimeter of a piece of felt and my last stitch will be right next to my first one, I like to leave 3" tails at the beginning and end of the line of stitches, then tie two overhand knots with the two tails, creating a square knot. See drawing at left.

It is best to tie knots on the wrong side of your work, or to hide them from view in some other way, such as sandwiching them between two layers of felt. Usually tying a knot twice will do the trick, but you might wish to add another knot or two to make sure that the stitches are secure. Be sure to trim the loose tails after you're done sewing.

Special Techniques

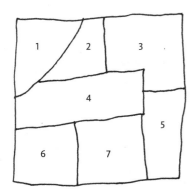

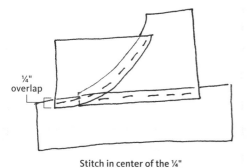

¼"
overlap

Stitch in center of the ¼"
overlap (⅛" in from edge)

PATCHWORK

Patchwork

Perhaps the best use of leftover scraps of felt is patchwork, which can be sewn into anything from pillowcases to curtains (see pages 88 and 96), potholders (see page 98), and large blankets. I prefer to create patchwork in one color family, mixing a variety of pastel and saturated colors, but it can also be stunning to use multicolored scraps, or even to use scraps of the same color stitched together with thread in a contrasting color.

To create patchwork, lay out a piece of newsprint 2" longer and wider than the size of the patchwork you plan to create (which accounts for the seams needed to sew the pieces together.) If your project has two sides, such as a pillowcase or potholder, you will need to create a front and a back. Making each side different will add visual interest, so you may wish to use two pieces of newsprint. Draw varying shapes onto your newsprint and write a number on each shape, in rows from left to right (see drawing at left) to indicate their placement. With paper scissors, cut out the shapes and pin them to felt scraps in your choice of colors. With fabric shears, cut out the felt pieces, leaving the pinned templates attached.

Lay out the fabric pieces according to the numbers and pin the felt pieces together, overlapping the edges by ¼". Be sure to consider which edges will go on top and which underneath before you begin sewing. Once all the pieces are pinned together, remove the paper. Sew the pieces together with a straight stitch and 2-ply embroidery floss, leaving about ⅛" between stitches, and working ⅛" from the edge. Leave tails at least 3" long at the edges so that if you need to trim the finished patchwork to a desired dimension, you can undo stitches at the edge, trim the excess fabric, and retie the knots at the new edge.

"Drawing" Stitches

Some of the projects in the book require that you stitch a design element, such as a face or a branch. Whether you create these elements using a template or sew them freehand is up to you.

DRAWING STITCHES WITH A TEMPLATE

To use a template for stitching, simply make an extra photocopy of the project template, reducing or enlarging the photocopy to the size indicated. Lay the photocopy directly over the area of felt where the design element will go and safety pin the paper in place. Thread your needle and stitch right through the paper, following the lines on the template to make an exact transfer. Carefully pull the paper away from the felt a little bit at a time as you sew. Do not pull directly up on the paper; remove the paper gently so as not to loosen or rip the stitches. When transferring satin stitches, which are often used for faces, stitch the general shape of the area to be filled in and then remove the template before piling on stitches (otherwise you will have to dig out the paper carefully with your needle).

Felt

Paper template

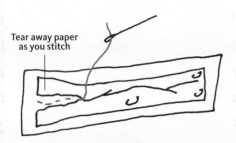

Tear away paper
as you stitch

**DRAWING STITCHES WITH A
TEMPLATE**

DRAWING STITCHES FREEHAND

I have always loved to draw with a fine-tipped pen or a sharp pencil, but I also enjoy drawing with freehand stitches as it produces some of the most surprising and organic results. I encourage you to give it a try as it is a nice way to capture your individual style.

When stitching freehand, I keep the sketch of what I am creating next to me as I work, which helps me understand the relationship between all of the elements in the design (the distance between a branch and the appliquéd bird that will sit on it, or the tilt of an appliquéd head, for example). Above all, I like to keep the design simple, focusing on the barest qualities, not the nitpicky details.

Stitching Natural Details Freehand

I often use straight stitches to draw natural elements, such as branches and flowers, and I try to imitate the imperfections of nature, letting a stray stitch become a twig that is angled roughly in the direction I am headed with my needle and thread. Once I have laid out my rough design in straight stitches, I go back and fill in the empty stitch spaces with double running stitches, making a solid line of stitches.

Stitching Faces Freehand

Among my favorite things to stitch freehand are faces, as no two faces ever wind up the same. And on more than one occasion, I have found that the expressions I have captured mimic my mood. In general, I like to set the eyes far apart and about one third of the way down from the top of the head. To start, I think of an emotion and the face that would express it—for example, a surprised face might have a circular mouth and eyes set higher than normal, whereas a sly face may have lower eyes set off center, mouth in a half smile. I prefer to draw expressions that are not simply smiling or frowning; using different expressions adds an endearing quality to the characters. Subtlety plays a large role in the finished expression, and a few stitches are sometimes all that is needed to fully express a mood—in fact, a slight shift in angle can entirely change an expression. I suggest drawing some faces with pencil and paper before you begin sewing, then, as you sew, stepping back every couple of stitches to see how the expression is shaping up.

PART 2

Projects

Picture Perfect Bunny Patch

I always enjoy creating an appliquéd patch to show off in one of the old frames I collect. I often hang groups of them in various sizes on a wall and admire the collection as a whole.

FINISHED DIMENSIONS
5" x 7"

MATERIALS

5" x 7" frame

5" x 7" dark blue felt, for boy background (pink felt, for girl background)

3½" x 3" white felt, for rabbit head/arms

2½" x 2" sky blue felt, for overalls (yellow felt, for dress)

2" x 1" brown felt, for boy shoes (green felt, for girl shoes)

Embroidery floss in white (for head/arms), orange (for stripes on overalls), purple (for stripes in dress), red (for mouth, nose, and girl shoes), aqua blue (for eyes and boy shoes)

Photocopy of Rabbit Patch template (page 119) and Elephant template (page 119), reproduced at 100%

STITCHES USED
Satin Stitch, Straight Stitch, Double Running Stitch, Whipstitch. Instructions for these stitches can be found on pages 14–15.

CUSTOM SIZING
To make a patch for a different frame size, cut the background felt to the same size as your frame backing, making sure the edges of the patch will be concealed by the frame. Reduce or enlarge the appliqué design on a photocopier to suit the patch size.

ALTERNATE TEMPLATES
This project can also be made with the Elephant template (page 119) or Giraffe template (page 117), reproduced at 100%.

1. Cut Appliqué Pieces

   With paper scissors, cut out the rabbit head/arms and overalls or dress from the Rabbit Patch template, and the shoe from the Elephant template. Pin the paper patterns to the felt pieces as designated in Materials and cut out the appliqué pieces with fabric shears. You will need to cut 2 shoes.

2. Assemble Appliqué Design

   Lay out the background fabric and assemble the rabbit, placing the head/arms first. Layer the overalls or dress on top of the arms, and tuck the shoes under the overalls or dress. Once you are happy with the layout and have ensured that the design fits nicely in the frame, temporarily secure the pieces with glue stick to the background.

   As you stitch decorative details onto the appliqué, always tie off the knots on the back side of the patch. Sew the eyes with 3-ply aqua blue floss using satin stitches. Sew the mouth and nose with 2-ply red floss, using satin stitches for the nose and straight stitches for the mouth. Using double running stitch and single-ply floss, stitch stripes in the overalls or dress. Using whipstitch and single-ply red floss, stitch the shoes. Whipstitch the head/arms with single-ply white floss.

3. Assemble Frame

   Apply glue stick to the backing of the frame and press the patch in place. Assemble the frame.

Business Card Holder

FINISHED DIMENSIONS
4½" x 3"

MATERIALS
4½" x 8" peach felt, for envelope

3½" x 2" mustard felt, for patch

2½" x 2" light pink felt,
for outer flower

1⅛" x 1" brick red felt,
for inner flower

Embroidery floss in brick red
(for pocket construction and
appliquéd patch) and light pink
(for inner flower and outer flower)

Photocopy of Botanical 1 template
(page 117), reproduced at 100%

STITCHES USED
French Knot, Straight Stitch,
Whipstitch, Blanket Stitch.
Instructions for these stitches
can be found on pages 14–16.

ALTERNATE TEMPLATES
This project can also be made
with the Bird on Branch template
(page 116) or Leaves template
(page 116), reproduced at 65%.

We operate a letterpress printer at Kata Golda, which is in and of itself a substantial and beautiful machine. But what it allows us to create is truly magical. With it, we are able to print on photo album, guest book, and journal covers, and also make our stationery and business cards. The first time I saw my own letterpress-printed business cards, I knew I needed a special place to keep them. Thus was born this quick and easy project.

1. Cut Appliqué Pieces

   With paper scissors, cut out the outer flower 1 and inner flower 1 pieces from the template. Pin the paper patterns to the felt pieces as designated in Materials and cut out the appliqué pieces with fabric shears.

2. Assemble Appliqué Design

   Stack the pink and brick red appliqué pieces to form a flower and place them on the mustard felt as shown in the photo at left. Temporarily secure each piece with glue stick.

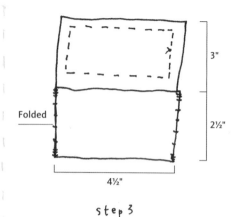

Folded

3"

2½"

4½"

step 3

Using 6-ply light pink embroidery floss, attach the inner flower to the outer flower by tying one French knot at each point of the inner flower, sewing through all 3 layers of felt. Do not cut the floss between knots. When you have sewn the French knots, sew a single straight stitch from each knot toward the center of the flower. Knot off on the back side once the final stitch is completed.

Using whipstitch and single-ply light pink floss, appliqué the outer flower to the mustard patch, spacing the stitches ¼" apart.

3. Create Pocket

Fold the peach felt piece to create a 2½"-deep pocket with a flap (as shown in the drawing at left). Secure both sides of the pocket with straight pins. With 3-ply brick red floss, knot off on the inside bottom corner of one side of the pocket and whipstitch 3 times close together around the corner edge. Then sew a blanket stitch along the pocket's side edge, spacing the stitches about ¼" apart. Whipstitch around the top corner edge 3 times close together and knot off on the inside.

Repeat on the other side of the pocket.

4. Attach Appliquéd Patch

Fold the flap down to close the pocket and temporarily secure the appliquéd patch in place with glue stick on the center of the flap.

With single-ply brick red floss, insert a needle from the wrong side of the flap, leaving a 3" tail, and straight stitch around the perimeter of the patch. When you have sewn around the entire patch, leave a 3" tail on the wrong side, secure the 2 tails with a square knot, and trim the loose ends.

olda

box 504
nd, Wa 98368
360 / 379 4714

information@katagolda.com

www.kata

kata go

post office box 5
port townsend, Wa

phone / fax 360 / 379

information@katagolda.com

www.katagolda.com

Photo Pocket

FINISHED DIMENSIONS
4½" x 7"

MATERIALS

7" x 13" light green felt,
for envelope

6" x 3" mint green felt, for patch

5½" x ½" dark green felt, for stem

4" x 1" white felt, for flowers

1" square dark purple felt, for dots

Embroidery floss in orange
(for appliquéd patch), red (for
pocket construction and French
knots), white (for flowers), dark
green (for stem), and brick red (for
connecting French knots
to flowers)

Photocopy of Botanical 2
template (page 117), reproduced
at 100%

STITCHES USED

Straight Stitch, Whipstitch, French
Knot, Double Running Stitch,
Blanket Stitch. Instructions for
these stitches can be found on
pages 14–16.

Holding a photograph in your hand is a special and
intimate treat, and it is especially rare these days, as so
many pictures are stored and shared digitally instead of
in an album. This pocket is a lovely way to keep a special
stash of photos on hand. It makes a perfect gift for
Grandma or for any other family member or friend who
appreciates this "old-fashioned" pleasure.

CUSTOM SIZING

This pocket is designed to hold
4" x 6" photographs. If your prints
are a different size, simply make
sure that the felt for the envelope
is 1" wider and three times taller
plus 1" taller than your photos.
You may need to enlarge or
reduce the template photocopy to
accommodate the new dimensions.

ALTERNATE TEMPLATES

This project can also be made with
the Bird on Branch template (page
116), Leaves template (page 116),
Snail template (page 118), or Dog
template (page 118), reproduced
at 100%.

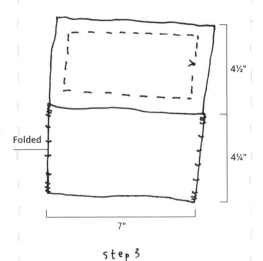

Folded

4½"

4¼"

7"

step 3

1. Cut Appliqué Pieces

   With paper scissors, cut out each shape from the template. Pin the paper patterns to the felt pieces as designated in Materials and cut out the appliqué pieces with fabric shears. You will need to make 8 of the purple dots.

2. Assemble Appliqué Design

   Assemble the appliqué design on the mint green felt patch as shown in the photograph on page 31. As you sew the appliqués in place, tie off all knots on the wrong side of the patch.

   First, temporarily secure the dark green stem to the patch using a glue stick. Using straight stitch and single-ply dark green embroidery floss, stitch around the perimeter of the stem.

   Arrange the white flowers on the stem with the smallest flower at the top, and temporarily secure them with glue stick. Using whipstitch and single-ply white floss, stitch around the flowers.

   Anchor each purple felt dot in place with a French knot using 6-ply red floss. With single-ply brick red floss and double running stitch, sew a line between each dot and the flower next to it.

3. Create Pocket

   Fold and pin the light green felt to create a 4¼"-deep pocket with a flap (as shown in the drawing above left). Secure both sides of the pocket with straight pins. With 3-ply red floss, knot off on the inside bottom corner of one side of the pocket and whipstitch 3 times close together around the edge. Then sew a blanket stitch along the pocket's side edge, spacing the stitches about ¼" apart. Whipstitch around the top corner edge of the pocket 3 times close together and knot off on the inside.

   Repeat on the other side of the pocket.

4. Attach Appliquéd Patch

Fold the flap down to close the pocket and temporarily secure the appliquéd patch in place with glue stick on the center of the flap.

With single-ply orange floss, insert a needle from the wrong side of the flap, leaving a 3" tail, and straight stitch around the perimeter of the patch. When you have sewn around the entire patch, leave a 3" tail on the wrong side, secure the 2 tails with a square knot, and trim the loose ends.

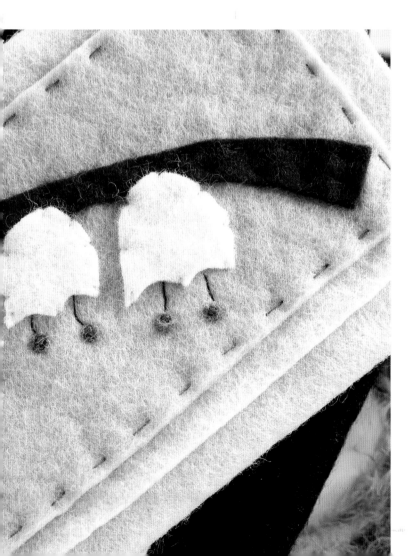

Glasses Case

FINISHED DIMENSIONS
2¾" x 6¾"

MATERIALS

8" x 10" sage green felt, for case

1½" x 2" mustard felt,
for outer leaves

1" x 1½" peach felt,
for inner leaves

Embroidery floss in rose
(for case, leaves, and button)
and brown (for stem)

¾" diameter button

Photocopy of Leaves template
(page 116), reproduced at 65%

STITCHES USED

Double Running Stitch,
Blanket Stitch, Straight Stitch.
Instructions for these stitches
can be found on pages 14–15.

ALTERNATE TEMPLATES

This project can also be made
with the Bird on Branch template
(page 116), reproduced at 65%.

Felt provides a layer of natural cushioning and is therefore an ideal material for protecting something as delicate as a pair of glasses. I tuck this case in a bag that goes with me everywhere and appreciate knowing that my glasses are safe and sound.

1. **Cut Case Felt and Appliqué Pieces**

   With fabric shears, cut two 2½" x 3½" pieces out of the corners of the sage green felt as shown in the drawing on page 36.

   With paper scissors, cut out the leaves from the template. Pin the paper patterns to the felt pieces as designated in Materials and cut out the appliqué pieces with fabric shears.

2. **Assemble Appliqué Design**

   Assemble the appliqué design on the sage green felt as shown in the drawing on page 36, with the peach inner leaves stacked on top of the mustard leaves. Make sure that all the leaves slant upward, with the largest ones at the bottom. Temporarily secure the pieces in place with glue stick.

As you complete the decorative stitches for the design during this step, tie off all knots on the wrong side of the felt. Stitch around each inner leaf ⅛" from the edge using double running stitch and single-ply rose floss. Connect the leaves with a branch by sewing stems with 2-ply brown floss and double running stitch (see page 19 for tips on stitching freehand). At each point where the leaf and stem meet, make a single stitch through all layers.

3. Sew Case

With the appliquéd side down, fold the sage green felt on the fold lines (see drawing below), tucking the right side under the left to create a top flap piece. With the flap up and out of the way, fold and pin the overlapped fabric in place. Starting at the bottom left corner, tie a knot on the inside of the sandwiched felt with 3-ply rose floss. Blanket stitch across the bottom of all 3 layers with stitches ¼" apart. Straight stitch up the seam on the right side through only two layers of felt, then to the left along the top opening, around the single-layer flap, and back to the opening on the right before knotting off on the inside.

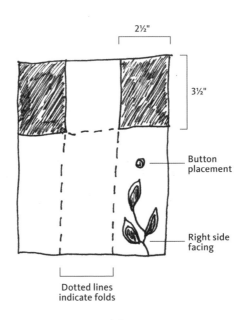

2½"

3½"

Button placement

Right side facing

Dotted lines indicate folds

Steps 1 and 2

4. Attach Button and Cut Buttonhole

Sew the button onto the center front of the case, 1½" below the opening. Fold the flap over the button and mark a ¾" horizontal slit for the buttonhole. Make sure that the button matches up with the slit before cutting the felt. Keep in mind also that the buttonhole should not be too large or loose, because the felt will stretch. Carefully cut the buttonhole open using the tip of fabric shears or small embroidery scissors. The hole should be roughly ⅛" smaller than the diameter of the button.

Pincushion

I use a variety of pins and needles when I work and this cylinder-shaped pincushion gives me enough room to organize them according to type and size. I always have a couple of pincushions going at the same time—one with all sorts of needles and one just for straight pins.

FINISHED DIMENSIONS
2½" x 4"

MATERIALS

7¼" x 3¾" rose felt,
for pincushion body

2½" x 1¼" orange felt,
for pincushion caps

3" x 1" lavender felt,
for outer flowers

2" x 1" sage green felt,
for inner flowers

Embroidery floss in brick red

Polyester fiberfill or wool stuffing

Photocopy of Botanical 1 template (page 117) and Pincushion Cap template (page 117), reproduced at 100%

STITCHES USED

French Knot, Straight Stitch, Whipstitch. Instructions for these stitches can be found on pages 14–16.

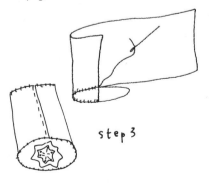

step 3

1. **Cut Appliqué Pieces**

   With paper scissors, cut out the outer flower 3, inner flower 3, and pincushion cap pieces from the templates. Pin the paper patterns to the felt as designated in Materials and cut out 2 of each piece with fabric shears.

2. **Assemble Appliqué Design**

   Assemble the appliqué designs on the pincushion caps by layering a green inner flower on a lavender outer flower on each orange piece of felt. Temporarily secure all 3 pieces with glue stick. Using 6-ply embroidery floss, tie French knots at each point of the inner flowers, then sew a single straight stitch from each knot toward the center of the flower, sewing through all 3 layers of felt.

3. **Sew Pincushion**

   Using single-ply floss and starting with the needle on the wrong side of the cap, attach the long edge of the rose felt to the cap using whipstitches about ⅛" apart (see drawing at left). Continue stitching the rose felt to the orange oval until you have stitched all the way along the edge of the rose felt piece—it will overlap itself a little bit at the end. Straight stitch through the overlapped rose felt to the other end of the pincushion.

   Attach the second pincushion cap the same way, pausing when there is a ½" opening to stuff the pincushion with fiberfill or wool stuffing. Once it is fully stuffed, finish whipstitching the cap into place. Knot off and tuck the knot under the edge of the cap so that it is not visible.

Little Girl's Puppy Purse

FINISHED DIMENSIONS

8" x 6" x 2" (without handles)

MATERIALS

8½" x 11" rose felt, for bag

Two pieces of 2" x 13" sage green felt, for handle

3½" x 3" brown felt, for dog

Embroidery floss in brick red (for purse construction and handle), light brown (for attaching dog body), dark brown (for nose), and aqua blue (for eyes)

Photocopy of Dog template (page 118), reproduced at 100%

STITCHES USED

Whipstitch, Straight Stitch, Double Running Stitch, Satin Stitch. Instructions for these stitches can be found on pages 14–15.

ALTERNATE TEMPLATES

This project can also be made with the Snail template (page 118) or Bird on Branch template (page 116), reproduced at 100%.

Durable enough to hold a rock collection, yet dainty enough to take to a tea party, this is the perfect accessory to make a little girl feel like a big girl. It's such a simple project that you could easily whip up a batch to hand out as favors at your little girl's next birthday party. If the guests are old enough, let each one choose her own appliqué and teach her how to sew it on all by herself.

1. **Cut Appliqué Pieces and Bag Felt**

   With paper scissors, cut out the dog body and ear from the template. Pin the paper patterns to the brown felt and cut out the appliqué pieces with fabric shears.

   With fabric shears, cut two 1" x 2" rectangles from the center of each long side of the rose felt, as shown in the drawing on page 42.

2. **Sew Bag Body**

   Fold the rose felt in half, lining up the short edges, and secure with straight pins. Using 3-ply brick red floss and starting at the base of the bag (just above the rectangle cut outs), tie a knot on the inside of the bag and sew 3 whipstitches close together. Straight stitch along the side of the bag. Sew 3 whipstitches close together at the top corner, and knot the thread on the inside. Repeat on the other side of the bag. (If the bag is uneven when you finish sewing the sides, you can fix it by trimming the top edge before knotting off.)

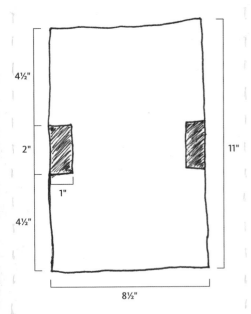

4½"

2"

1"

4½"

11"

8½"

Step 1

Pinch the bottom of one side of the bag base to create a flat edge perpendicular to the side seam. Tie a knot on the inside of the bag and sew 3 whipstitches close together at the corner of the bag base. Straight stitch across the base, making sure to stitch through the bag's side seam, where the base and sides meet (see drawings below left). At the other corner of the base, sew 3 whipstitches close together, then knot off on the inside. Repeat on the other side of the bag base.

3. Prepare and Attach Handles

Fold one handle piece lengthwise and, using 3-ply brick red floss and straight stitch, stitch down the length of the felt, creating a 1" x 13" tube. Tie knots at the beginning and end of the stitching on the same side of the tube. Repeat for the other handle piece.

Position a handle on the upper outside edge of the bag, 1" from the top and 1" in from the left side. With double running stitch, sew an X across the handle end, tying off the knots on the inside of the bag. Attach the other end of the handle on the right-hand side in the same manner, making sure not to twist the handle.

Use safety pins to attach the second handle temporarily to the opposite side of the bag so that you can make sure the bag hangs correctly. Adjust the placement as needed, then repeat the steps above to permanently attach the second handle.

4. Appliqué Dog

Using satin stitches, sew eyes on the dog appliqué with 3-ply aqua blue floss; sew the nose with 3-ply dark brown floss.

Position the dog body and ear on the bag and temporarily secure them with glue stick. Using single-ply light brown floss, whipstitch the perimeter of the dog body, then sew around the dog ear, tying off the knots inside the bag.

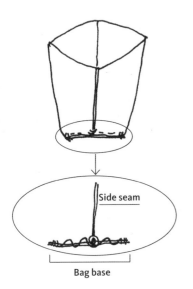

Side seam

Bag base

Step 2

Stuffed Animal Family

FINISHED DIMENSIONS
11" x 7" x 1"

MATERIALS
See chart below, plus polyester fiberfill or wool stuffing, and photocopy of Stuffed Animal Dog, Mouse, or Rabbit templates (pages 120–125), reproduced at 100%.

These dolls are enjoyed by kids and adults alike—I've even been told that their "open-to-interpretation" expressions remind some people of their favorite childhood pets. Whether you make a dog, mouse, or rabbit, I hope you enjoy personalizing the faces of these stuffed animals as much as I do.

MATERIALS	Dog Girl	Dog Boy	Mouse Girl	Mouse Boy	Rabbit Girl	Rabbit Boy
Head, Outer Ears, & Body	24" x 7½" tan felt	24" x 7½" tan felt	24" x 7½" light gray felt	24" x 7½" light gray felt	24" x 7½" white felt	24" x 7½" white felt
Inner Ears	3" x 3" rose felt	3" x 3" rose felt	3" x 3" light pink felt	3" x 3" light pink felt	3" x 3" peach felt	3" x 3" peach felt
Shirt	15" x 4½" rose felt	12" x 4" dark blue felt		10½" x 5" orange felt		12" x 4" mint green felt
Skirt/Dress/Pants	12" x 4" pale yellow felt	10" x 4" sage green felt	11" x 6¾" pale yellow felt	10" x 4" forest green felt	12½" x 7" light pink felt	10" x 4" light brown felt
Collar	3½" x 1½" orange felt	3½" x 1½" yellow felt	3" x 1½" rose felt	3" x 1½" mint green felt	3½" x 2¼" mint green felt	
Embroidery Floss	Dark brown (for eyes, mouth, and nose), tan (for animal construction), rose (for shirt), pale yellow (for skirt), and orange (for collar)	Dark brown (for eyes, mouth, and nose), tan (for animal construction), dark blue (for shirt), sage green (for pants), and orange (for collar)	Dark brown (for eyes), red (for mouth and nose), light gray (for animal construction), pale yellow (for dress), and rose (for collar and French knots)	Dark brown (for eyes), red (for mouth and nose), light gray (for animal construction), orange (for shirt), mint green (for collar), and dark green (for pants)	Aqua blue (for eyes), red (for mouth and nose), rose (for swirl in ears and X's on dress), white (for animal construction), light pink (for dress), and mint green (for collar)	Aqua blue (for eyes and X's on shirt), red (for mouth and nose), rose (for swirl in ears), white (for animal construction), mint green (for shirt) and light brown (for pants)

STITCHES USED

Satin Stitch, Double Running Stitch, Blanket Stitch, Whipstitch, French Knot. Instructions for these stitches can be found on pages 14–16.

1. Cut Template Pieces

With paper scissors, cut out all of the template pieces. Pin the paper patterns to the felt pieces as designated in Materials and cut out 1 of collar piece (if applicable) and 2 of all the other pieces with fabric shears.

2. Stitch Face

You may wish to freehand stitch the face design using your own inspiration; if so, see the tips on page 19. If you would rather stitch the face using the template as a guide, pin the paper head pattern to the felt and stitch through the paper (see page 18 for more on this technique). Stitch the eyes and nose using 6-ply floss and satin stitch. Stitch the mouth using 2-ply floss and double running stitch. Tie knots on the wrong side of the face.

3. Assemble Head

Lay the head pieces with the wrong sides together, lining up the ear locations. Lay the inner ears on top of the outer ears. For the mouse and rabbit only, make a small tuck in the center of the narrow end of the ear. For the dog only, pinch the narrow end of the ears in half so that they fold slightly. Pin the 2 layered ears to the head at the ear locations, sandwiching their edges between the stacked head pieces. Check to make sure that the ears are facing in the same direction. The fold in the dog ears should face forward and slightly down.

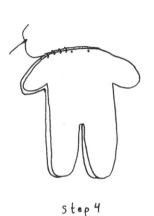

step 4

Starting at the neck edge, sew the head pieces together using 2-ply floss and blanket stitch. Sew double running stitch across the ears to attach them securely. Stitch around the entire head, stopping at the other neck edge, and knot off on the inside of the head. For the rabbit only, stitch a "swirl" through the inner and outer ear using a double running stitch and 2-ply floss. Tie knots on the backside of the double-layer ear.

4. Sew Body

Lay the 2 body pieces on top of each other and transfer the dots from the template to the neck edge with marker. Starting at the neck edge, sew around the entire body using 2-ply floss and blanket stitch, leaving an opening between the dots at the neck edge (see drawing at left). Knot off on the inside of the body.

5. Stuff Body and Head

Stuff the head and body firmly with fiberfill or wool stuffing. The legs and arms should be extra firm; only the torso should feel soft. Add extra stuffing to the neck area on the head and body.

6. Attach Head to Body

Insert the body opening into the head opening, overlapping the edges ½". With 2-ply floss, starting at the middle-back neck edge of the body, whipstitch the head to the body. Sew around the entire neck and tie a secure knot, hiding the knot between the head and body.

7. Attach Clothing

Temporarily secure the collar (if applicable) on the front neck edge of the shirt or dress with glue stick. Using 6-ply floss, join the pieces with 5 French knots (for dog) or whipstitches (rabbit and mouse), spaced evenly across the collar. Set aside.

Lay the skirt or pants pieces on top of each other and sew blanket stitch up one side of the garment with 2-ply floss. Be sure to knot the thread securely at the beginning and end of the seam. Slip the garment onto the doll and sew the other side together. The top of the skirt or pants should be about 1" from the arms, and the bottom should be about 1" from the feet. For the pants, sew blanket stitch around the inner legs, as well.

Attach the shirt or dress using 2-ply floss in the same way you attached the skirt and pants, sewing along both side and shoulder seams. Make sure that the collar is in the front and that the bottom of the shirt overlaps the top of the pants or skirt.

Holds Everything Bucket

FINISHED DIMENSIONS

Small bucket: 7½" wide x 15" tall before top is rolled

Large bucket: 10" wide x 15" tall before top is rolled

MATERIALS

Small bucket: 7½" circle tomato felt, for base; 22½" x 15" sky blue felt, for sides; 23" x 1½" gold felt, for stripe

Embroidery floss in red

Large bucket: 10" circle dark brown felt, for base; 30" x 15" mint green felt, for sides; 23" x 2" red felt, for stripe

Embroidery floss in bright pink

STITCHES USED

Blanket Stitch, Straight Stitch. Instructions for these stitches can be found on pages 14–15.

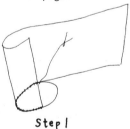

Step 1

Step 2

These buckets are a perfect storage solution for everything from embroidery floss and buttons to tiny toys to rolled-up magazines. I like to line up three or four of them in different colors and sizes to create a lovely yet functional display.

1. Attach Base to Sides

Using 6-ply embroidery floss, knot off on the edge of the circle and attach the circle to the long edge of the side piece using blanket stitch with stitches ½" apart (see drawing at left). Sew until the circle is completely attached and the ends of the bucket sides overlap roughly 1½". The overlap fabric will be covered by the stripe in the next step.

2. Sew Stripe Over Bucket Seam

Safety pin one end of the stripe on the outside of the bucket to cover the overlapping fabric that forms the side seam, aligning the stripe so that the end is even with the bucket's base. Arrange the stripe so that it covers the full 15" seam, and wrap the remaining stripe fabric over the bucket top to cover about half the seam on the inside of the bucket. Safety pin the other end of the stripe in place. (I find it helpful to hold the bucket up to the light to make sure that the stripe lines up on the inside and outside.)

Using 2-ply floss, knot off on the top inside edge of the bucket and straight stitch around the perimeter of the stripe, sewing through all layers of felt (see drawing below left). It is important to start sewing at the top of bucket because you may need to trim off some excess stripe at the base after stitching. Knot off on the inside of the bucket and trim the bottom edge of the stripe if it is too long. Roll down the top edge in order to make the bucket stand.

Gift Wrap Tag

These unique tags are so endearing that some recipients may temporarily forget to wonder what's *inside* the gift to which they've been affixed. They're also a great way to use leftover felt scraps.

FINISHED DIMENSIONS

35" x ½" strap (for a box
10" long x 7" wide x 1½" tall)
Strap lengths will vary depending on size of gift.

MATERIALS

Two pieces 35" x ½" pink felt (or a ribbon), for straps

1" x 3" rose felt, for flowers

2½" square gold felt,
for snail shell

3½" x 2" grass green felt,
for snail body

2" circle 80-lb cream-colored paper, for tag

Embroidery floss in brown (for flowers and eyes) and red (for gift card and mouth)

Photocopy of Botanical 2 template (page 117) and Snail template (page 118), reproduced at 100%

STITCHES USED

Satin Stitch, Straight Stitch. Instructions for these stitches can be found on pages 14–15.

CUSTOM SIZING

If your gift is a different size, simply make sure that each strap is long enough to leave 4" tails once it has been wrapped around the gift.

ALTERNATE TEMPLATES

This project can also be made with the Botanical 1 template (page 117), Bird on Branch template (page 116), or Leaves template (page 116). Reproduce the template at a size that will suit the package you are wrapping.

1. Cut Appliqué Pieces

   With paper scissors, cut out 3 flowers of varying sizes and the snail shell and body from the templates. Pin the paper patterns to the felt pieces as designated in Materials and cut out the shapes with fabric shears.

2. Embellish Straps

   Wrap each strap around the box to ensure that it is the correct length and trim accordingly (I like the tails to be about 4" long after wrapping).

   Attach a flower to 3 of the strap ends using single-ply brown floss and a single straight stitch secured with a square knot.

   Stitch a face freehand onto the snail body, referring to the template. (If you wish to sew a different face on the snail, see the tips on page 19). Stitch the eyes with 3-ply brown floss and small satin stitches, and sew the mouth with single-ply red floss and a single straight stitch.

   Write your message on the cream-colored paper and temporarily secure it onto the snail shell with glue stick. Glue the bottom edge of the snail shell to the body. Straight stitch around the perimeter of the paper (through the snail shell, body, and paper) with single-ply red floss.

On the backside of the snail, sew the snail onto the remaining undecorated strap end using single-ply brown floss and a single straight stitch secured with a square knot.

3. Wrap Gift

Wrap one of the felt straps around the gift once and tie a square knot on top of the box. Then wrap the other felt strap around the box on the other two sides and tie a knot.

Stationery Pouch

FINISHED DIMENSIONS

4¾" x 6½" (for a set of six
4" x 6" cards and envelopes)

MATERIALS

18" x 6½" brown felt, for pouch

Salmon felt: 3½" x 2½" (for pencil
pocket) and 2" x 6½" (for spine)

Embroidery floss in cream

STITCHES USED

Whipstitch, Straight Stitch,
French Knot. Instructions for
these stitches can be found on
pages 14–16.

Being a letter writer, I treasure my stationery pouch and love the way it feels in my hand as I saunter off to find a place to write. I've included pockets for two writing utensils, stamps, paper, and envelopes. If you prefer email to handwritten letters, this pouch could also be used to organize household receipts and bills, or even as a wallet.

1. Sew Pouch

   Fold the short sides of the pouch 3¾" toward the center and secure the edges with straight pins (see drawing on page 56).

   Using 2-ply embroidery floss, knot off on the inside of the pocket at a folded corner and sew 3 whipstitches close together. Stitch through both layers of fabric along the edge of the pocket using straight stitch until you reach the pocket opening, then whipstitch 3 times close together. With the same strand, continue to straight stitch along the open edge of the pocket, taking care to only sew through that single layer of fabric. Whipstitch at the opposite corner 3 times and straight stitch through both layers of fabric to close up the other side of the pocket (see stitching lines in drawing on page 56). Finish with 3 final whipstitches to secure the seam. Repeat to sew the pocket at the other end of the pouch.

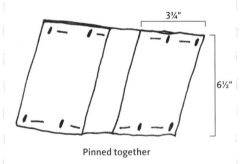

3¾"

6½"

Pinned together

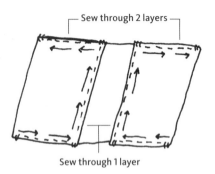

Sew through 2 layers

Sew through 1 layer

Step 1

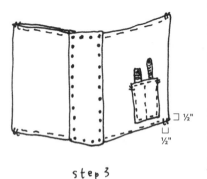

½"

½"

step 3

2. Sew Spine

Close the pouch like a book, center the salmon felt spine on the outside of the pouch, and safety pin it in place. With 6-ply floss, sew a French knot every ½" around the perimeter of the spine, being careful to stitch through only the spine and one layer of the brown felt (otherwise you will stitch the interior pockets closed). Do not cut the floss between French knots; this will create a line of straight stitches on the insides of the pouch pockets.

3. Sew Pencil Pocket

With the stationery pouch closed, safety pin the pencil pocket into place on the front of the pouch ½" from the lower right corner.

Starting at the top left corner of the pencil pocket and using 2-ply floss, knot off on the back side (i.e., the inside of the stationery pouch pocket) and straight stitch 2 horizontal stitches to secure the pencil pocket edge. Be sure to stitch through only 2 layers of fabric (not all 3)—otherwise, you'll sew right through your interior pocket. Straight stitch down the left side of the pencil pocket, across the bottom, and up the right side, then sew 2 horizontal stitches at the top right corner to secure it. Straight stitch across the top of the pencil pocket, sewing through that layer of felt only. Then straight stitch a vertical line down the center of the pocket, sewing through 2 layers of felt to create holders for 2 pencils (see drawing at left). Knot off in the interior of the stationery pouch.

A Fetching Portfolio

FINISHED DIMENSIONS
9¼" x 11¾" (for
8½" x 11" documents)

MATERIALS
Dark brown felt: 24" x 18" (for
case) and ½" circle (for button)

Lavender felt: 9" x 11½" (for
interior back piece), 7½" x 3¼"
(for flap); and 38" x ½" (for strap)

7½" x 3¼" gold felt, for flap

8½" x 11" piece of ⅛"-thick
mat board

Embroidery floss in brown

STITCHES USED
Straight Stitch. Instructions
for this stitch can be found on
page 14.

I like to transport the flat work I create—such as
illustrations, stationery, or photos—in a portfolio case.
The hard back keeps the papers from bending, and the
water-resistant wool felt protects the work against coffee
spills or unexpected rain. I especially enjoy thinking about
what I will put in a portfolio before I start making one and
then choosing felt colors to complement those contents.

1. **Cut Case Felt**
   With fabric shears, cut a 7½" x 3¼" rectangle from each corner of the dark brown
   felt (see drawing at left).

2. **Attach Interior Back Piece**
   Sandwich the mat board between the brown felt and the 9" x 11½" lavender felt,
   making sure the board is centered. Safety pin the edges of both fabrics. Starting
   on the brown side, straight stitch around the perimeter of the lavender felt using
   2-ply floss. Tie the thread tails in a square knot on the brown side when completed.

24"

18"

3¼"

7½"

Step 1

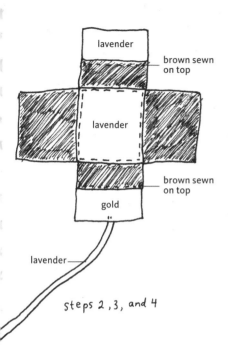

lavender

brown sewn on top

lavender

brown sewn on top

gold

lavender

steps 2, 3, and 4

3. Attach Flaps

Position the gold flap partially under one of the short brown pieces that extends from the lavender center, overlapping the edges by ¼" (see drawing at left). Secure the flap with straight pins and straight stitch through both layers of fabric with 2-ply floss, tying the knots on the brown side.

Repeat on the other short side with the lavender flap.

4. Attach Tie Closure

At the center edge of the gold flap, sandwich the lavender strap between the brown felt circle and the flap. Starting on the wrong side of the flap, stitch an X through all 3 layers and tie off on the wrong side with a square knot.

To close the portfolio and tie it shut, see the drawing below left.

step 4

Everyday Journals

FINISHED DIMENSIONS

Large journal: 4½" x 6"

Small journal: 4½" x 3"

MATERIALS

Large journal:

Six 8½" x 11" sheets 80-lb cream-colored paper

9¼" x 6" oatmeal felt, for cover

Blue felt: Two pieces 4¼" x 5½" (for patches inside cover) and 3" x 2" (for bird)

Embroidery floss in green (for book construction), blue (for bird), dark brown (for branch), brown (for eye), and red (for beak)

Photocopy of Bird on Branch template (page 116), reproduced at 100%

Small journal:

Three 8½" x 11" sheets 80-lb cream-colored paper

9¼" x 3" pink felt, for cover

2½" x 1½" mint green felt, for outer leaves

Gold felt: Two pieces 4¼" x 2¾" (for patches inside cover) and 2½" x 1½" (for inner leaves)

Embroidery floss in mint green (for book construction) and forest green (for stem and leaves)

Photocopy of Leaves template (page 116), reproduced at 65%

Both journals:

Pencil

Awl (or large, sturdy needle)

Bone folder (or dull edge of a butter knife)

STITCHES USED

Double Running Stitch, Whipstitch, Satin Stitch, Straight Stitch. Instructions for these stitches can be found on pages 14–15.

ALTERNATE TEMPLATES

This project can also be made with the Botanical 2 template (page 117), reproduced at 65% for small journal and 100% for large journal. Or include a pencil pocket on the front cover of the large journal as described in Step 3 of the Stationery Pouch on page 56.

Some say these journals are too pretty to write in, but I say they're too pretty *not* to write in. Whether you're jotting down a list of things to do, a quote from a book, or recording a memory, this is a lovely way to chronicle the passage of time and the unfolding of life.

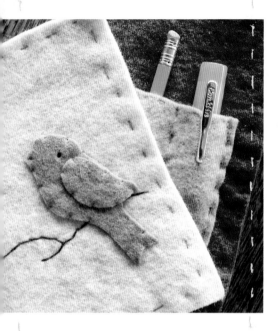

1. **Cut Appliqué Pieces**

   With paper scissors, cut out the template pieces. Pin the paper patterns to the felt pieces as designated in Materials and cut out the appliqué pieces with fabric shears.

2. **Stitch Design Details**

   BIRD DESIGN

   Using a double running stitch and 3-ply dark brown embroidery floss, stitch a branch across the width of the cover felt. Either freehand stitch the branch design using your own ideas or using the template as a guide (see page 19 for tips about freehand work) or pin the photocopy of the template to the felt and stitch through the paper (see page 18 for more on this technique). Knot off on the wrong side of the work.

   Fold the cover in half (to its finished dimensions) and place the bird body on the front cover directly over the branch, as shown in the photograph at left and on page 62. Temporarily secure it in place with glue stick, then whipstitch around the entire shape using single-ply blue floss. Place the wing on the body and whipstitch around the perimeter of the wing. Using 3-ply brown floss and small satin stitches, sew the eye. Sew the beak with 3-ply red floss and a single straight stitch.

   LEAVES DESIGN

   Sew stem and appliqué across the width of the cover felt as described in Steps 2 and 3 of the Glasses Case on pages 35–36; the appliqués should appear on the front cover only.

3. **Sew Patches Inside Cover**

   Open the journal cover and lay the patches on the inside front and back covers about ¼" from the edges. Temporarily secure the patches in place with glue stick. Using single-ply floss, insert the needle from the patch side, leaving a 3" tail, and straight stitch around the perimeter of the patch. When you have sewn around the entire patch, leave a 3" tail on the wrong side and tie both tails in a square knot. Trim the ends once the knot is secure. Repeat on the other inside cover.

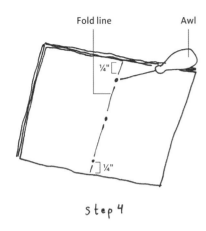

Fold line   Awl

¼"

¼"

step 4

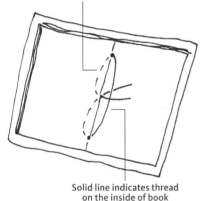

Dotted line indicates thread
on the outside of book cover

Solid line indicates thread
on the inside of book

Step 5

4. Prepare Journal Pages

Stack the sheets of paper and fold them in half (to 8½" x 5½"). Crease the fold with a bone folder and tear it one sheet at a time.

LARGE JOURNAL ONLY
Restack the torn paper and fold it in half once more to make pages that are 4¼" x 5½". Crease the fold with a bone folder to create a pamphlet.

SMALL JOURNAL ONLY
Restack the torn paper and fold it in half to 8½" x 2¾". Crease the fold with a bone folder and tear the sheets again. Restack the paper and fold it in half one last time to create a pamphlet with pages that are 4¼" x 2¾". Crease the fold with a bone folder.

BOTH JOURNALS
Open the pamphlet to the center fold and mark 3 equidistant points with pencil on the inside of the fold; the top and bottom points should be about ¼" from the edge.

Using an awl or sturdy needle, stab through 4 sheets of paper at a time (see drawing at left). Use your pencil marks as a guide, placing the sheet with the marks on top of the unpunched sheets and repeatedly piercing through the same holes. Take care to pierce directly through the fold.

5. Attach Pages to Cover

Open the cover and center the pages inside it. Open the journal pages to the center fold.

Thread a needle with a strand of 3-ply floss that is about 2½ times the height of the pamphlet. Following the drawing at left, insert the needle from the inside center hole through to the outside cover, leaving a 3" tail. Check that the pamphlet is positioned correctly, then bring the needle back to the inside through the top hole, down through the bottom hole to the outside, and back to the inside of the journal through the center hole. Tie the 2 tails in a square knot, catching the long thread that travels between the top and bottom holes in the knot.

Terra-Cotta Pot Cozy

FINISHED DIMENSIONS
15¼" x 3½" (to fit a 5½" diameter terra-cotta pot)

MATERIALS
15¼" x 3½" dark blue felt, for cozy

5" x 2" light green felt, for outer leaves

5" x 2" sage green felt, for inner leaves

7" x 1" mint green felt, for ties

Embroidery floss in light green (for stem), forest green (for inner leaves), and dark blue (for darts)

Photocopy of Leaves template (page 116), reproduced at 100%

STITCHES USED
Straight Stitch, Double Running Stitch. Instructions for these stitches can be found on page 14.

Wool has many amazing qualities, and two of its best are used in this project. Not only will this cozy keep the roots of your plant warm in cooler months, but wool's moisture-wicking properties will prevent water from evaporating through the terra-cotta, keeping the soil moist. And of course, a hand-stitched cozy adds a whimsical touch to any plant display.

CUSTOM SIZING
This pattern can be easily adapted to a pot of any size. I prefer to use pots that have a lip at the top edge because it provides an edge for the cozy to butt against. To determine the height of the cozy, measure the pot from the bottom of the lip to ½" above the bottom of the pot. To determine the width of fabric needed, measure around the pot just beneath the lip, then add 2½".

ALTERNATE TEMPLATES
This project can also be made with the Bird on Branch template (page 116), or Botanical 1 or 2 templates (page 117), reproduced at 100%.

1. Cut Appliqué Pieces

With paper scissors, cut out the template pieces and pin them to the felt pieces as designated in Materials. With fabric shears, cut out 2 of inner and outer leaf 1, 2 of inner and outer leaf 2, and 1 of inner and outer leaf 3.

2. Assemble Appliqué Design

Stack the corresponding outer and inner leaf pieces and temporarily secure them with glue stick. Lay out the assembled leaves on the blue felt background, with larger leaves on one end of the cozy and smaller leaves on the other end. Do not position leaves within 2½" of the side edges of the background felt. Alternate the direction of the leaves so that they point at roughly 45-degree angles toward the top and bottom of the pot. See the photo at left and the drawing below for suggested layouts.

When you are happy with the layout of the leaves, temporarily secure them on the blue felt with glue stick. Using a straight stitch and single-ply forest green embroidery floss, stitch ⅛" inside the perimeter of the inner leaves to secure the appliqué pieces.

Using double running stitch and 2-ply light green floss, stitch between the bases of the leaves to freehand stitch a stem, with the largest leaves at the base of the stem. Make one stitch in the base of each leaf appliqué (through all 3 layers) where the leaf connects to the stem. (For tips on freehand stitching natural elements, see page 19.)

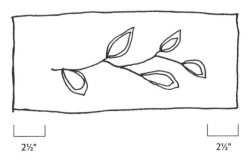

2½"   2½"

step 2

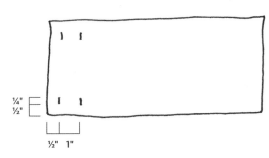

¼"
½"

½" 1"

step 3

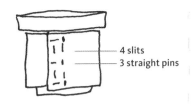
4 slits
3 straight pins

step 3

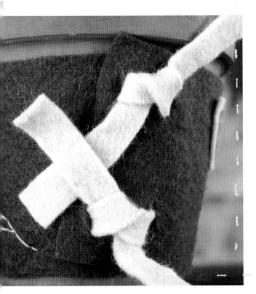

3. Make Ties and Cut Holes

Cut the mint green felt in half lengthwise, creating two 7" x ½" strips.

Using the tip of fabric shears, make 2 pairs of vertical slits at one end of the blue background felt as shown in the drawing on the opposite page.

Wrap the cozy snugly around the pot just beneath the lip, overlapping the edge with the slits on the outside. (The cozy will not be snug at the bottom if the pot is tapered—you'll fix that in the next step.) Pin the overlapping edges together and carefully insert the tip of the fabric shears through the slits you already made, cutting 4 corresponding slits at the opposite end of the cozy (see drawing at left).

Remove the pins and fasten the cozy to the pot by lacing the mint green strips through the slits and and tying the ends together in a basic overhand knot (see drawing at left and photograph at bottom left).

4. Add Darts to Bottom of Cozy

With the cozy on the pot, mark locations for 3 darts, evenly spaced along the bottom edge. Fold the felt at the dart locations and pin in place vertically, making sure that the bottom of the cozy fits snugly. Remove the cozy from the pot and open it out flat. Sew 3 horizontal straight stitches through each dart ¾" from the bottom edge with 2-ply dark blue floss, knotting off on the wrong side (see drawing below).

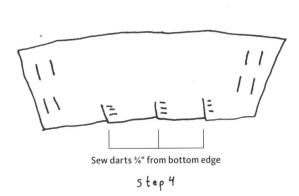

Sew darts ¾" from bottom edge

step 4

Songbird Mug Cozy and Coaster

FINISHED DIMENSIONS
13" x 3⅛" (to fit a 3⅜"
diameter x 3¾" tall mug)

MATERIALS
13" x 3⅛" light orange felt,
for cozy

Dark brown felt: 13" x 3⅛"
(for cozy lining) and two 3½"
circles (for coaster)

2" x 3" red felt, for birds

1" x 3" brick red felt, for wings

Embroidery floss in brown (for
branch), red (for birds and
wings), and light blue (for eyes
and cozy construction)

¾" button

Photocopy of Bird on Branch
template (page 116), reproduced
at 65%

Photocopy of Bird on Branch
template (page 116), reproduced
at 50%

Just as a wool sweater will keep you warm on a chilly day,
this cozy will keep your drink warm as you work your way
through the morning paper or a stitching project. And
because it has a built-in coaster, it can be set down safely
on any surface between leisurely sips.

STITCHES USED
Double Running Stitch, Whipstitch,
Satin Stitch, Straight Stitch.
Instructions for these stitches can
be found on pages 14–15.

CUSTOM SIZING
It's easy to adjust the size of the
cozy to fit your favorite mug. To
determine the height of the fabric
needed, make the cozy ½" to 1"
shorter than the cup's height. To
determine the length of fabric
needed, measure the diameter of
the mug, multiply it by 3½, and
add 1". Cut out the coaster pieces
so they are ⅛" larger than the
diameter of the mug.

ALTERNATE TEMPLATES
This project can also be made
with the Botanical 2 template
(page 117) or Leaves template
(page 116), reproduced at 100%.

1. Cut Appliqué Pieces

   With paper scissors, cut out the two sets of bird and wing template pieces and pin them to the felt pieces as designated in Materials. With fabric shears, cut out the appliqué pieces, then pin and cut one more set of the larger bird and wing.

2. Trim Cozy to Fit Mug

   Wrap the orange felt rectangle around the mug and trim the left edge so that the cozy will fit through the handle (see drawing below). Holding the strip in place through the handle, trim the top and bottom edges as needed so that ½" to 1" of mug shows at the top of the cozy, and roughly ⅛" shows at the bottom.

3. Assemble Appliqué Design

   Using a double running stitch and 3-ply brown embroidery floss, stitch a branch across the cozy. Either freehand stitch the branch design using your own ideas or using the template as a guide (see page 19 for tips about freehand work) or pin the photocopy of the template to the felt and stitch through the paper (see page 18 for more on this technique). Knot off on the wrong side of the felt.

   Next, position the bird bodies and wings onto the branch on the cozy (see drawing below for suggested placement), and temporarily secure them with glue stick. Using single-ply red floss, whipstitch the birds and then the wings to the background. Referring to the template as a guide, mark a dot on each bird with permanent marker to make an eye. Stitch the eyes with 3-ply light blue floss, using satin stitch.

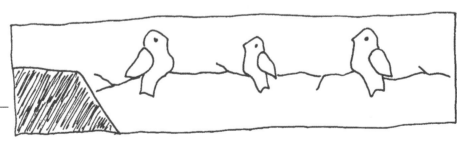

Trim for handle

Steps 2 and 3

Start whipstitch here

Step 5

Step 6

4. Sew Cozy Lining

Trim the dark brown felt rectangle to the same size as the orange felt and lay the 2 pieces with wrong sides together. Starting on the brown side with single-ply light blue floss, leave a 3" tail and straight stitch around the perimeter of the cozy. Tie a square knot on the brown side.

5. Attach Coaster

Stack the 2 dark brown felt circles. Connect them to the bottom edge of the cozy using single-ply light blue floss and whipstitch. Start at the straight edge of the handle and stitch around the perimeter, connecting coaster to cozy. When you get back to the handle area, continue the line of whipstitches around the rim of the double-layered coaster, even though there is no cozy to sew through (this will give a finished look). Knot off inside the cozy at the same place you began.

6. Attach Button

Using permanent marker, make a dot in the center of the thin section of cozy that slips through the handle. Sew the button on the dot and tie off with a square knot on the wrong side. Wrap the cozy around the mug snugly and mark the spot where the buttonhole should go. Make a vertical slit for the buttonhole using the tip of fabric shears. Because felt stretches, the hole should be roughly ⅛" smaller than the diameter of the button.

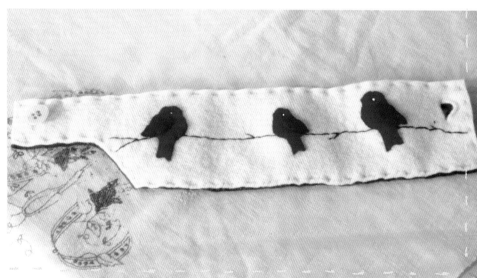

Finger Puppets and Puppet Bed

FINISHED DIMENSIONS
1¾" x 3¼" (not including tail)

MATERIALS
Light gray felt: 2½" x 5½" (for body and outer ears) and 7" x ½" (for tail)

1½" x ¾" red felt, for inner ears

Embroidery floss in light gray (for mouse construction, ears, and tail), brown (for eyes and nose), and red (for mouth)

Photocopy of Mouse Finger Puppet template (page 118), reproduced at 100%

STITCHES USED
Satin Stitch, Straight Stitch, Double Running Stitch. Instructions for these stitches can be found on pages 14–15.

CUSTOMIZING
The template given is for a mouse, but you can easily create other animals by adjusting the ear shapes, facial features (such as whiskers for a cat), and tail length.

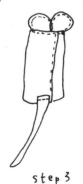

step 3

Finger puppets are a great way to put leftover scraps of felt to use. Plus they're quick to make and provide a fun opportunity to experiment with stitches, facial expressions, shapes, and colors. And when it's time to put your finger puppets to bed, tuck them into a sweet puppet holder, as shown on page 77.

Mouse Finger Puppet

1. Cut Appliqué Pieces

With paper scissors, cut out the template pieces. Pin the paper patterns to the felt pieces as designated in Materials and cut out the shapes with fabric shears. You will need 2 of each inner and outer ear.

2. Stitch Mouse Face

Using satin stitches and 2-ply embroidery floss in the colors designated in Materials, stitch the face freehand. Refer to the template or see the tips on page 19, if you wish to create a different face.

3. Construct Puppet

Stack the inner ear pieces on top of the outer ear pieces. Fold the mouse body to form a finger puppet, overlapping the edges by ½". Sandwich each ear between the front and back of the puppet, with the inner ear facing forward, and pin all layers in place.

Using single-ply light gray floss, tie a knot on the inside of the puppet's upper right back corner and straight stitch through all layers across the top of the puppet (front, ears, and back overlap). Once the ears are attached, stitch around the inner ears, then, on the backside, stitch the overlapping gray felt down to the base of the puppet. Attach the tail with double running stitch and tie off inside.

FINISHED DIMENSIONS

12" x 8½", with five
2¼" x 2½" pockets

MATERIALS

12" x 11" mint green felt, for case

½" x 20½" dark purple felt,
for strap

Dark brown embroidery floss

STITCHES USED

Whipstitch, Straight Stitch.
Instructions for these stitches
can be found on pages 14–15.

Puppet Bed

1. Fold and Sew Case

Lay out the mint green felt and fold the long bottom edge up 2½" (see drawing below). Pin the fold in place, then place pins at equal distances across it to create five 2¼" wide pockets.

Starting at the bottom right edge, tie a knot on the inside of the pocket and sew 2 whipstitches using 2-ply floss. Straight stitch up to the upper right edge of the pocket and whipstitch twice. Continuing in straight stitch, sew up the right side of mint green felt, across the top, and down the left side. When you reach the top left pocket edge, sew 2 whipstitches, straight stitch down the pocket, and sew 2 more whipstitches at bottom left edge before knotting off on the inside of the pocket.

To form the inner pockets, knot off on the inside bottom of a pocket, then straight stitch up to the pocket edge, removing pins as you go. Sew 2 horizontal straight stitches at the top of each pocket opening and knot off inside the pocket. Repeat for the remaining pockets.

2. Attach Strap

Attach the strap directly above the pocket opening on the outside of the case (see drawing below). Sew it in place using 3-ply floss and 3 straight stitches. Knot off on the inside of the flap.

3. Put Puppets to Bed

Tuck the puppets into the pockets, fold the top flap over them, and loosely roll up the case toward the strap. Wrap the strap around the roll and secure it.

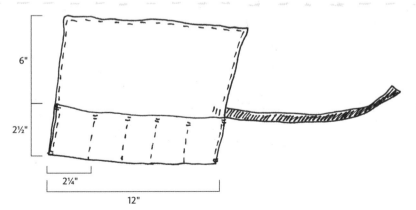

6"

2½"

2¼"

12"

steps 1 and 2

step 3

Tooth Fairy Pillow

This adorable pillow will get used over and over again as your little one loses baby teeth. Instead of tucking the tooth under a bed pillow for the Tooth Fairy to pick up, your child can hold the pillow like a favorite stuffed animal. And rest assured, it provides a safe and secure pocket to tuck the tooth into—an important feature, since tiny teeth are easy to misplace.

1. **Cut Appliqué Pieces**

   With paper scissors, cut out the template pieces (for the pink pillow, use the star and wand templates from the 80% photocopy, and the pocket template from the 100% photocopy). Pin the paper patterns to the felt pieces as designated in Materials and cut out the appliqué pieces using fabric shears.

2. **Assemble Appliqué Design on Pocket**

   For the pink pillow, arrange the star and wand on the pocket as shown in the photo at right, placing the star just over the tip of the wand. For the blue pillow, arrange the star and moon on the pocket as shown in the photo at right. Temporarily secure the pieces in place with glue stick. Using single-ply light brown embroidery floss, knot off on the wrong side and straight stitch down the center of the wand. Using single-ply yellow floss and always knotting off on the wrong side of the felt, make a stitch at each star point, from the point toward the center. Using single-ply white floss, knot off on the wrong side and whipstitch around the perimeter of the moon.

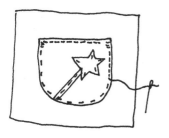

Stitch through 2 layers of felt around sides, bottom, and at top corners of pocket, but through 1 layer of felt across pocket opening

step 2

Center the pocket on one of the pink or blue felt squares and safety pin it in place. Starting at the upper right corner of the pocket, with 3-ply floss, knot off on the back side and sew 2 horizontal stitches to secure the pocket edge. Straight stitch down the right side, across the bottom, and up the left side, then sew 2 horizontal stitches at the top left corner. Straight stitch across the open edge of the pocket, sewing through that layer of felt only, and knot off on the wrong side. Then, using 3-ply floss in second color, sew along the same path you followed with the first floss, alternating stitches to create a 2-color double running stitch. See the stitch lines in the drawing at left.

3. Sew Pillow

Align the felt squares on top of each other, with the appliqué design on the outside. Knot off on the wrong side and sew a two-color double running stitch, as described in Step 2, around the pillow, leaving about half a side open so you can insert the stuffing.

Stuff the pillow, making sure to push the stuffing into the corners, so that it fills evenly. Stop when you are happy with the feel of the pillow—I like to make mine as full as possible. (An overstuffed pillow will also help keep the tooth snugly in the pocket.)

Finish sewing around the perimeter of the pillow and tie the tails in a square knot to secure the threads, tucking the tails between the pillow front and back to hide them.

Mail Pocket

FINISHED DIMENSIONS
18" x 14"

MATERIALS
18" x 14" purple felt, for wall hanging front

18" x 14" yellow felt, for wall hanging back

8" x 6" red felt, for pocket

8" x 6" orange felt, for pocket

White felt: 18" x 3" (for letters) and three ½" x 7" strips (for loops)

Embroidery floss in purple (for pockets and lettering) and mint green (for perimeter of wall hanging and loop attachment)

Photocopy of the Alphabet template (page 115), reproduced at 200%

STITCHES USED
Whipstitch, Straight Stitch. Instructions for these stitches can be found on pages 14–15.

I originally designed this wall hanging for my little girl after she started to read and write and began to enjoy sending and receiving letters. As it turned out, we all made use of the big organizational pockets, so this wall hanging has become a permanent fixture in our home.

1. Cut Appliqué Pieces

With paper scissors, cut out the letters needed to spell *mail, in,* and *out* (*a, i, l, m, n, o, t,* and *u*). Pin the paper patterns to the white felt and cut out the letters using fabric shears. You will need 2 of the letter *i*.

2. Assemble Appliqué Design

Center the word *in* on the red felt. Center *out* on the orange felt. Center *mail* at the top of the purple felt, with the tallest letter ½" from the top edge. Temporarily secure all letters in place with glue stick, then whipstitch around the perimeter of each one (as well as along the inside edge, where applicable) with single-ply purple floss, keeping the stitches roughly ½" apart. Knot off the tails at the beginning and end of each letter and tie a square knot on the wrong side.

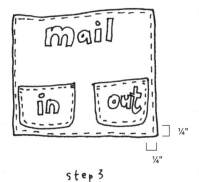

¼"

¼"

step 3

3. Attach Pockets to Background

Set each pocket ¼" from the bottom and side edges of the purple felt (see drawing at left) and safety pin them in place. Starting at the upper left corner of a pocket and using 3-ply purple floss, knot off on the back side and sew 2 horizontal stitches to secure the edge. Straight stitch down the left side, across the bottom, and up the right side, and sew 2 horizontal stitches at the top right corner to secure it. Straight stitch across the open edge of the pocket, sewing through that layer of felt only, and knot off on the wrong side of the purple felt.

Repeat to attach the second pocket.

4. Attach Backing

Lay the purple wall hanging front, with the pockets facing up, on top of the yellow back. Using straight stitch and 3-ply mint green floss, knot off between the 2 layers and straight stitch around the perimeter of the wall hanging. Knot off on the wrong side, tucking the tails between the layers.

5. Create Hanging Loops

Attach the 3 loops at the top edge of the wall hanging (one at each corner and one centered) by sandwiching ½" of finished wall hanging between the loop ends and stitching an X with 6-ply mint green floss. Knot off on the back side of the wall hanging.

mail

in

out

Odette's Door Sign

FINISHED DIMENSIONS

3" x 26¾" (for a 6-letter sign)

MATERIALS

3" yellow circles (2 for each letter in sign)

2" x 2½" red felt pieces, for letters (1 for each letter in sign)

1" x 30" purple felt strip (see Custom Sizing for adjusting length)

Embroidery floss in light blue (for letters) and red (for circles)

Photocopy of the Alphabet template (page 115), reproduced at 200%

STITCHES USED

Whipstitch, Straight Stitch. Instructions for these stitches can be found on pages 14–15.

We all like to mark our own special space, and here is an easy way to do just that. Thanks go to Kimberly Augustine for making the prototype as a gift for my daughter, Odette. Kimberly's clever work gave me the idea to create all sorts of door signs, which can spell out any name, or even a message such as "Welcome," "Open," "Closed," or "WC."

CUSTOM SIZING

The length of your sign will depend on how many letters you wish to use. To determine how much purple felt you need, do the following calculation:

___ letters x 3" = ___" (for circles)

+ ___ spaces between letters x ½" = ___"

+ 9½" for loop at top and tail at bottom

= ___" (length of purple strip)

A standard doorknob is mounted 36" from the floor, so if you want to use more than 8 letters, you will need to reduce the size of the circles and letters—or hang the sign from something higher than a doorknob.

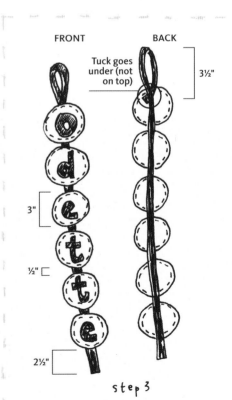

FRONT   BACK

Tuck goes under (not on top)

3½"

3"

½"

2½"

step 3

1. Cut Appliqué Pieces

   With paper scissors, cut out the template pieces you need for your sign and pin them to the red felt pieces. With fabric shears, cut out the appliqué pieces.

2. Assemble Appliqué Design

   Temporarily secure each letter to a yellow circle with glue stick. Whipstitch the letters onto the circles using single-ply light blue embroidery floss and spacing the stitches ½" apart. Leaving a tail, start sewing on the back side of the circle and whipstitch around the perimeter of each letter (as well as the inner edge, where applicable). Knot off the tails at the beginning and end of each letter in a square knot.

3. Assemble Sign

   Stack each appliquéd yellow circle on top of a blank yellow circle and temporarily secure in place with glue stick.

   Fold one end of the purple felt strip over 3½", making a loop. Position the top center edge of the circle with the first letter for the sign over the loose end of the loop; safety pin all 4 layers in place. Continue pinning letters in place along the strip, spacing the circles ½" apart (see drawing at left). Using straight stitch and single-ply red floss, stitch around the perimeter of each circle, making sure to sew through both the circle and the purple strip at the top and bottom. Tie off the tails on each circle on the back side with a square knot.

Textured Pillows

FINISHED DIMENSIONS

13½" square

MATERIALS

12" square pillow insert

Three size-4 sew-on snaps

Elephant pillow:

Rose felt: 13½" square (for pillow front) and 1½" x 5" (for snap covers)

Yellow felt: 13½" square (for pillow back) and 7" square (for snap covers, elephant jacket, and sleeve)

5" x 3" pink felt, for skirt or shorts

5" x 6" gray felt, for head, ear, and hands

½" x 3" dark blue felt, for shoes

Embroidery floss in aqua blue (for snaps, snap covers, border, and skirt or shorts), yellow (for jacket, sleeve, and shoes), red (for jacket and mouth), brown (for eyes and eyebrows), and gray (for head, ear, and hands)

Photocopy of Elephant template (page 119), reproduced at 200%

Whether in a child's room or in a sitting room, a colorful pile of textured pillows makes a nice visual impact.
I like to mix and match appliquéd animal pillows with patchwork pillows in the same tones, and enjoy how the irregular shapes in the patchwork and the playful shapes of the animals complement one another.

Patchwork pillow:

Scraps of felt to make two 13½" square pieces in different hues of red, for patchwork

Six 1½" sage green felt circles, for snap covers

Embroidery floss in light blue (for patchwork) and brick red (for border, snaps, and snap covers)

STITCHES USED

Satin Stitch, Straight Stitch, Double Running Stitch, Whipstitch. Instructions for these stitches can be found on pages 14–15.

CUSTOM SIZING

To adjust the size of your pillowcase, measure the length and width of the pillow you would like to cover and add 1½" to each measurement.

ALTERNATE TEMPLATES

This project can also be made with the Rabbit Patch template (page 119) or Giraffe template (page 117), reproduced at 200%.

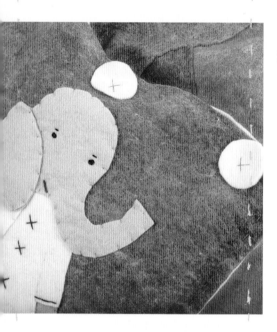

1. **Cut Elephant Pillow Appliqué Pieces**

   With paper scissors, cut out the template pieces and pin them to the felt pieces as designated in Materials. Using fabric shears, cut out the appliqué pieces. Make sure to plan ahead before you cut so that you do not run out of felt. You will need 1 each of the head, ear, sleeve, jacket, and skirt or shorts pieces; 2 each of the shoes and hands; and 3 rose and 3 yellow pieces cut into 1½" circles for the snap covers.

2. **Create Pillow Front and Back**

   PATCHWORK PILLOW

   Using the red scraps and light blue floss, follow the patchwork instructions on page 17 to make two 13½" square patchwork pieces.

   ELEPHANT PILLOW

   Lay out the appliqué pieces on the rose background, beginning with the shoes, then adding, in order, the skirt or shorts, jacket, sleeve, and head; each piece should overlap ⅛". Tuck the hands ⅛" under the sleeves and cuffs. Place the ear on the head over its existing ear to create a "doubled" ear layer. Temporarily secure all pieces with glue stick.

   Mark small dots for eye placement with permanent marker. Satin stitch the eyes and straight stitch eyebrows right above them with 6-ply brown embroidery floss. Using 6-ply red floss, stitch the mouth with a single long stitch. Refer to the template for placement of all facial features, or see page 19 for tips on freehand sewing other types of facial expressions. Be sure to tie off all knots on the wrong side of the rose felt.

   With 6-ply red floss, make 3 X's down the front of the jacket, creating each X by sewing 2 long straight stitches that cross each other in the middle. Sew cuffs onto the sleeves with red floss using a double running stitch. Make sure, as you do this, to sew through the hands, which are tucked beneath the sleeves.

¼"

To create the decorative pattern on the skirt, stitch 4 rows of arrowheads, pointing up, using 2-ply aqua blue floss. (The arrowheads are created by sewing pairs of long straight stitches at right angles to each other.) If you don't have room to create a full arrowhead at the edge of the skirt, simply sew a single slanted stitch. To stitch vertical stripes in the shorts, use double running stitch and single-ply aqua blue floss.

Using single-ply gray floss, whipstitch around the edges of the head, ear, and hands. With single-ply yellow floss, whipstitch around the edges of the jacket, sleeves, and shoes. All whipstitches should be spaced approximately ½" apart. With yellow floss, sew a double running stitch from the trunk down to the cuff to define the right sleeve.

3. Sew Pillowcase

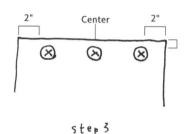

2"   Center   2"   ¾"

step 3

Lay the two patchwork pieces on top of each other with wrong sides together, or lay the appliqué pillow front on top of the yellow pillow back with the pattern facing up. Straight stitch down one side, across the bottom, and up the other side using 3-ply floss, tying knots at the beginning and end of the stitching on the inside of the pillowcase. Stitches should be about ¼" in from the edge, ¼" long, and ¼" apart (see drawing at left).

Using 2-ply floss, attach 3 snaps to the inside front of the pillowcase about ¾" from the top edge. The side snaps should be 2" in from the edge, and the third snap should be centered between them (see drawing at left). Sew the corresponding snap pieces onto the other inside edge of the pillowcase. For the elephant pillow, attach the rose snap covers to the yellow background and the yellow covers to the rose background by sewing an X in the center of each circle using 2-ply floss and 2 long straight stitches. Attach sage green snap covers to the patchwork pillow in the same way. Knot off as close to the snap as possible on the inside of the pillowcase.

Insert the pillow into the case and close the snaps.

Baby's Giraffe Quilt

FINISHED DIMENSIONS
34" square

MATERIALS
Mint green felt: 34" square
(for quilt back) and 17" square
(for quilt front)

17" square lavender felt,
for quilt front

Yellow felt: Two 17" squares
(for quilt front) and 11" x 7"
(for giraffe body)

Two 2½" circles rose felt,
for quilt center

1" x 7" dark brown felt, for dots

Embroidery floss in rose (for
quilt border), forest green (for
piecing quilt top and attaching
center circles), mint green (for
attaching quilt top to quilt back),
dark brown (for tail, hoofs, and
dots), yellow (for giraffe body),
red (for giraffe nose), and aqua
blue (for giraffe eyes)

Photocopy of Giraffe template
(page 117), reproduced at 200%

When it comes to baby accessories and toys, I'm always
drawn to simplicity. Watching my own daughter grow,
I loved seeing her respond to basic animal shapes,
colors, and faces. This blanket is designed to engage
the baby's imagination while in use as a warm covering
or play mat.

STITCHES USED
Satin Stitch, Whipstitch, Double
Running Stitch, Straight Stitch,
Blanket Stitch. Instructions for these
stitches can be found on pages 14–15.

ALTERNATE TEMPLATES
This project can also be
made with the Rabbit Patch
template (page 119) or
Elephant template (page
119), reproduced at 200%.

1. Cut Appliqué Pieces

   With paper scissors, cut out the template pieces and pin them to the felt pieces as designated in Materials. With fabric shears, cut out the giraffe body and dots.

2. Assemble Giraffe Appliqué

   Place the giraffe body on the lavender felt, then position the dots on the body, as shown on the template, trimming the dots as needed. Temporarily secure the pieces in place with glue stick.

   Freehand stitch the hoofs, eyes, nose, and tail as follows, using the template as a guide.

   Using 6-ply embroidery floss, satin stitch hoofs onto the feet with dark brown floss, the eyes with aqua blue floss, and the nose with red floss. Using single-ply yellow embroidery floss, whipstitch the giraffe body to the background with stitches spaced ½" apart. Using double running stitch and 6-ply brown floss, stitch the tail, making first stitch into giraffe body.

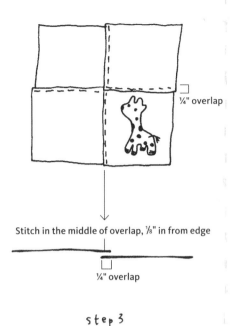

¼" overlap

Stitch in the middle of overlap, ⅛" in from edge

¼" overlap

s t e p 3

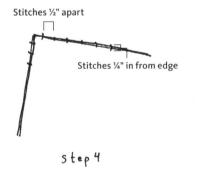

Stitches ½" apart

Stitches ¼" in from edge

s t e p 4

3. Assemble Quilt Top

Lay out the 4 quilt top squares with each square overlapping the one next to it by ¼" (see drawing at left for suggested layout and overlap). Safety pin the squares together, using 3 pins to attach each side. Using 2-ply forest green floss, straight stitch the squares together ⅛" from the edge, removing the safety pins as you go. Secure the knots on the wrong side of the work at the beginning and end of the stitching line. Don't worry if the center of the quilt looks unfinished at this point—it will be hidden by the rose circle appliqués in the next step.

4. Attach Quilt Top to Backing

Lay the quilt top on the mint green backing with the appliqué facing upward. Smooth out the fabric and safety pin the pieces together along the stitched lines. Using 2-ply mint green floss, sew a double running stitch along the existing stitched lines, filling in the spaces between the forest green stitches. The effect will be a simple mint green straight stitch on the back of the quilt and a double running stitch with alternating colors on the front. Remove the safety pins and smooth out the fabric as you stitch.

Using glue stick, temporarily secure the rose circles on the center of the front and back of the quilt, aligning the circles so they are stacked one on top of the other. Using 2-ply forest green floss, sew a straight stitch around the perimeter of both circles at the same time ⅛" from the edge, tying square knots at the beginning and end of the stitching line on the back side of the quilt. You will be sewing through 4 layers of felt the whole way, which requires a bit of patience. Take your time and check to make sure that your stitches look nice on both sides of the quilt.

Smooth the quilt out flat. Trim the edges if the front and back sides are not even. (I am more concerned about the shape and feel of the quilt than I am about creating a perfect square.) Using 6-ply rose floss, blanket stitch the perimeter of the quilt. The stitches should be roughly ½" apart and ¼" from the edge (see drawing at left). Check frequently to make sure that the front and back sides continue to match up evenly (you may need to trim as you work). When you run out of a strand of thread, tie a new strand to the old one using a square knot and continue working in blanket stitch. It looks best if the knot lands between 2 stitches so that the tails can be easily tucked inside the quilt.

Patchwork Curtain

FINISHED DIMENSIONS

31" x 32" (not including loops), to cover a 30" square window

MATERIALS

Felt scraps in 5 different hues of red, for patchwork

7" x 10" pink felt, for loops

Embroidery floss in light blue (for curtain construction) and brick red (for loops)

1" curtain rod

STITCHES USED

Straight Stitch. Instructions for this stitch can be found on page 14.

CUSTOM SIZING

You can easily adapt these instructions to accommodate whatever materials you have on hand, and whatever size window you want to dress. See page 17 for instructions on how to design your own patchwork.

The loops at the top of the curtain should be spaced evenly.

When I make patchwork, I stick to one color family and play around with different tones, mixing and matching the pieces to see which arrangement best distributes the light and dark shapes. I have patchwork curtains in shades of green in my bedroom year-round, and in the winter I hang red curtains in my glassed-in front porch. When light shines through the curtains, the room is infused with a soft glow that makes me feel warm and cozy.

1. Create Patchwork Piece

   Using the felt pieces and light blue floss, follow the patchwork instructions on page 17 to make a 31" x 32" patchwork piece. Cut seven 1" x 10" strips of pink felt for loops.

2. Create and Attach Loops

   Lay out the 7 curtain loops along the top of the patchwork piece, spacing them approximately 4½" apart. Fold each loop over so that it sandwiches the top patchwork edge by 1" on each side. With 6-ply brick red floss, sew 3 horizontal straight stitches in the 1" overlap of each loop, sewing through all layers. Tie all knots on the wrong side of the curtain.

3. Hang Curtain

   Trim the thread tails and slide the curtain onto the rod. Hang it with the right side of the curtain facing inside the room. If the curtain is too long, trim the bottom edge, following the instructions on page 17.

Patchwork Potholder

FINISHED DIMENSIONS

7¾" square

MATERIALS

Yellow potholder:

4 pieces 8" x 4" felt in different hues of yellow, for patchwork and loop

2" x 31" rose felt, for binding

Embroidery floss in green (for patchwork and loop) and brick red (for binding)

8" square cotton quilt batting

Green potholder:

4 pieces 8" x 4" felt in different hues of green, for patchwork and loop

2" x 31" brick red felt, for binding

Light pink embroidery floss

8" square cotton quilt batting

STITCHES USED

Straight Stitch. Instructions for this stitch can be found on page 14.

I use patchwork to make a variety of items, from table runners to curtains (see page 96) to wrappings for fragile and special gifts. But this patchwork potholder is one of my favorites because it is not only beautiful and functional, but is also a trusted tool for my nine-year-old baker and me. Though it may require a bit more time to create than some of the other projects in this book, it is well worth the effort.

1. Create Patchwork Pieces

   Using the patchwork felt pieces and following the patchwork instructions on page 17, make 2 patchwork pieces, each 7¾" square, for the front and back of the potholder. Cut an 8" x 1" piece from the patchwork felt of your choice for the loop.

2. Assemble Potholder

   Sandwich the batting between the wrong sides of the 2 patchwork pieces. Trim the edges so that all sides line up before you bind them together.

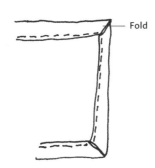
— Fold

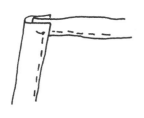

Step 2

Wrap the binding around each edge of the sandwich so that half falls on each side of the potholder, pinning it in place as you wrap. Fold the binding over on itself as you round the corners (see drawing at left), just as you might tuck a corner when making a bed. Sew the binding to the potholder with a straight stitch, using 2-ply embroidery floss and making sure to sew through all layers. When the binding is attached all the way around the potholder, overlap the binding edges and knot off the thread.

3. Create and Attach Loop

Fold the 8" x 1" strip of felt lengthwise and sew a straight stitch using 2-ply embroidery floss, creating a tube. Tie knots at the beginning and end of the stitching line on the same side of the tube.

Attach the loop to the corner of the binding where the stitch line began and ended (see drawing below left). Sew one side of the loop on each side of the finished binding using 2-ply embroidery floss and being careful not to twist the loop. Stitch 4 times through all layers to secure the loop, and finish by tying a square knot between the potholder and loop. Hide the loose thread ends.

Tie knot between potholder and back of loop

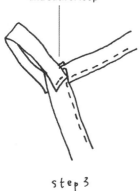

step 3

Messenger Bags

FINISHED DIMENSIONS
Kid's bag: 12" x 10½"
Adult bag: 14" x 13"

MATERIALS
Kid's bag:

12" x 32½" lavender felt, for bag front, back, and flap

Four 3¼" x 28½" pieces mint green felt, for sides/strap

Yellow felt: 5½" x 6" (for large pocket) and two 4½" x 5" pieces (for smaller pockets)

2½" square white felt, for rabbit head/arms

2" x 2¼" pink felt, for dress

1" square purple felt, for shoes

Embroidery floss in rose (for bag, sides/strap, pockets, mouth, nose, and shoes), purple (for front pocket), forest green (for rabbit eyes), grass green (for stripes in dress), white (for rabbit head/arms)

1" square of sew-on Velcro

Photocopy of the Rabbit Patch template (page 119) and Elephant template (page 119), reproduced at 80%

Adult bag:

14" x 28" gray felt, for bag body

Four 3½" x 33" pieces brick red felt, for sides/strap

Tomato red felt: 14" square (for bag flap); 7" x 6" (for back exterior pocket); 2" x 5½" (for interior pocket); 4" square (for interior pocket); two 2¾" x 4" pieces (for side pockets)

Embroidery floss in aqua blue

1¾" button

This bag is very popular with both kids and adults. The wide strap on the kid's version fits nicely over a child's shoulder and is comfortable for lugging books to school, while the adult version is perfect for people like me who tend to carry around stitching projects, books, and journals. Both bags have pockets for pens, keys, and anything else you might need to find quickly. If you're making the bag as a gift, have your intended recipient pick out the colors or appliqué, and if the bag needs some reinforcement after extended use, rest assured that additional stitches only give it more character.

STITCHES USED
Satin Stitch, Straight Stitch, Whipstitch, Double Running Stitch. Instructions for these stitches can be found on pages 14–15.

ALTERNATE TEMPLATES
For the Kid's Bag, this project can also be made with the Elephant template (page 119) or Giraffe template (page 117), reproduced at 80%, or the Dog template (page 118) or Snail template (page 118), reproduced at 100%.

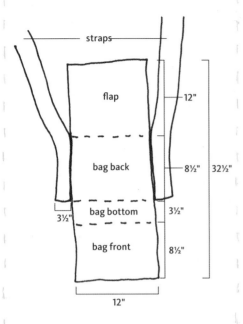

straps

flap

12"

bag back

8½"   32½"

bag bottom   3½"

3½"

bag front   8½"

12"

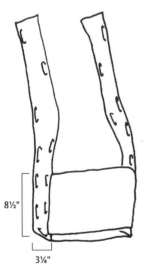

8½"

3¼"

step 3

Kid's Messenger Bag

1. Cut Appliqué Pieces

With paper scissors, cut out the rabbit head/arms and overalls from the Rabbit Patch template, and the shoe from the Elephant template. Pin the paper patterns to the felt pieces as designated in Materials and cut out the shapes with fabric shears. You will need to cut 2 shoes.

2. Assemble Appliqué Design

Assemble the appliqué pieces on one of the 4½" x 5" pieces of yellow felt, laying down the head/arms first, then the dress. (Note that the ears will hang over the top edge of the yellow felt.) Bring the left arm up and over the dress, and tuck the shoes underneath the dress. Once you are happy with the layout, temporarily secure the pieces with glue stick and glue the assembled rabbit to the background.

You may wish to freehand stitch the eyes, nose, and mouth using your own ideas or using the template as a guide (see page 19 for tips). Alternatively, lay the paper template onto the felt, pin it in place, and stitch through the paper (see page 18 for more on this technique).

Using the colors designated in Materials, satin stitch the eyes and nose with 3-ply embroidery floss. Stitch the mouth with single-ply floss and single straight stitches. Use double running stitch and single-ply grass green floss for the stripes in the dress. Whipstitch the shoes, head, and arms using single-ply floss in the colors designated. Tie off all loose threads on the back side of the patch.

3. Assemble Bag and Straps

Lay out the lavender felt; measure 12" from one short end and mark this measurement with safety pins on both sides. This 12" will serve as the bag's flap.

Arrange 2 pieces of mint green felt one on top of the other and safety pin them together to make a double-layer strap. Repeat with the remaining 2 pieces of mint green felt. Starting at the 12" marked measurement, place a double-layer green side/strap piece along each side of the lavender felt (see drawing at top left). Safety pin 8½" of lavender felt and side/strap together. Then fold

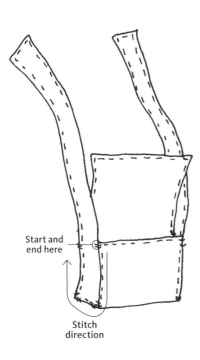

Start and
end here

Stitch
direction

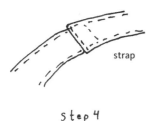

strap

step 4

the lavender felt and safety pin it to the 3½" bottom of the side/strap. Fold the lavender felt over and safety pin it for 8½" along the opposite side of the green felt (see drawing at bottom of opposite page). Repeat the same process on the other side of the lavender felt using the remaining double-layer piece of mint green felt. You have now assembled the body of the bag.

Leave the flap loose so that it can hang over the front of the bag; it should fall about ½" shy of the bottom edge (this may require trimming once you have assembled and sewn the bag).

4. Sew Bag and Straps

Using 3-ply rose embroidery floss, knot off on the top inside front of the bag (not the flap). Sandwich the knot between the double-layer strap and the bag body and whipstitch 3 times close together. Straight stitch along the front of the bag down to the base, attaching the side/strap. Whipstitch twice at the side base of the bag, whipstitch twice on the bottom of the bag, then straight stitch across the bottom of the bag, whipstitch twice at the bottom and twice at the side base, then continue in straight stitch up the back of the bag. Whipstitch 3 times at the top back corner, where the flap will begin. Continue straight stitching along the edge of the strap and straight stitch down the other side of strap to the top inside front of the bag, where you began (see drawing at top left for more detail). Knot off securely on the inside of the bag.

Repeat the same process on the opposite side of the bag.

Straight stitch along the 3 loose sides of the flap (not the fold line), knotting off inside the bag. Then straight stitch along the top front side of the bag (beneath the flap), again knotting off inside.

Overlap the ends of the straps and pin in place at the desired length. Straight stitch around the perimeter of the overlap (see drawing at bottom left).

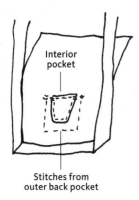

Interior
pocket

Stitches from
outer back pocket

Back
pocket

Step 5

5. Attach Velcro and Pockets

VELCRO

Safety pin the loop side of the piece of Velcro in place on the back side of the flap, 2½" from the bottom edge. With 3-ply purple floss, straight stitch around the perimeter of the Velcro. Close the flap to determine proper placement for the other half of the Velcro on the bag body, and attach it as for the first piece.

FRONT POCKET

Safety pin the appliquéd pocket in the center of the front flap, 1¼" from the bottom edge, making sure to cover the stitch line created when you attached the Velcro. Starting at the upper left corner of the pocket and using 3-ply rose floss, knot off on the back side and sew 2 horizontal stitches to secure the pocket edge. Straight stitch down the left side of the pocket, across the bottom, and up the right side, and sew 2 horizontal stitches at the top right corner to secure it. Straight stitch across the open edge of the pocket, sewing through that layer of felt only and carrying the thread behind the rabbit ears, and knot off on the wrong side. Switch to 3-ply purple floss and sew along the same path, alternating stitches to create a 2-color double running stitch.

INSIDE AND BACK POCKETS

Safety pin the smaller pocket to the inside center back of the bag (see drawing top left) and stitch it in place with 3-ply rose floss and straight stitch, just as you did for the front pocket (but omitting the 2-color double running stitch).

Safety pin the larger pocket on the outside center back of the bag (see drawing at bottom left), concealing the stitch line from the interior pocket, and stitch it in place as for the smaller interior pocket.

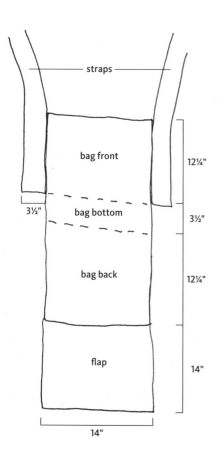

— straps —

bag front

12¼"

3½"   bag bottom   3½"

bag back

12¼"

flap

14"

14"

Step 1

Adult Messenger Bag

1. Assemble Bag and Straps

Arrange 2 of the brick red side/strap pieces one on top of the other to make a double-layer strap. Repeat with the remaining 2 pieces of brick red felt.

Lay out the gray felt; measure 12¼" from one short end and mark this measurement with safety pins on both sides.

Place one end of a double-layer side/strap at one of the marked points. Safety pin the brick red and gray felt pieces together along the 12¼" edges. Pin the second side/strap on the other side edge in the same way.

Working one side at a time, fold the unpinned gray felt around the brick red felt, securing it with safety pins first to the 3½" bottom edge of the strap, then up along 12¼" of the other side of the strap (see drawing at left). Repeat the same process on the other side using the remaining double-layer strap. You have now formed the body of the bag.

Secure the tomato red felt square to one open side of the gray felt with safety pins to create a flap. (The tomato red felt should overlap the gray felt on the outside of the bag.)

2. Sew Bag and Straps

Using 3-ply floss, knot off on the top inside front of the bag (where the flap and gray bag body meet). Sandwich the knot between the strap and bag body and whipstitch 3 times close together. Straight stitch across the flap to the other edge. Sew 3 whipstitches close together and knot off on the interior of the bag. The flap should hang over the front of the bag, about ½" shy of the bottom edge (this may require trimming once you have assembled and sewn the bag).

Sew the bag and sides/strap together as in Step 4 of the Kid's Messenger Bag on page 105. If you would like to make your strap longer, use a third piece of double-layer strap fabric to bridge the two side/straps together.

3. Attach Pockets and Button

INTERIOR POCKETS

Safety pin the 2" x 5½" and 4" square pieces of tomato red felt inside the bag on the center back. Keep in mind that both pockets must fit within the area that will be covered by the 7" x 6" exterior back pocket (see drawing at left). Starting at the upper left corner of one pocket and using 3-ply floss, knot off on the inside of the pocket and sew 2 horizontal stitches to secure the edge. Straight stitch down the left side of the pocket, across the bottom, and up the right side, then sew 2 horizontal stitches at the top right corner to secure it. Straight stitch across the open edge of the pocket, sewing through that layer of felt only, and knot off on the wrong side. Repeat for the second interior pocket.

STRAP POCKETS

Center the small pockets on each strap, one 5½" from the bag base, and the other ¾" from the bag base (see drawing at left). Safety pin and sew them in place as for the interior pockets.

BACK EXTERIOR POCKET

Safety pin the 7" x 6" tomato red felt on the bag back, covering the stitch line visible from sewing the interior pockets (see drawing at left). Sew the pocket in place as for the interior pockets.

BUTTON

Close the flap over the bag body and mark a spot 3½" from the bottom edge of the flap and centered along the width. Mark the same spot on the bag front beneath the flap, and attach the button to this spot with 3-ply floss. With the tip of fabric shears, carefully cut a vertical slit at the marked location in the flap for the buttonhole. Make the hole roughly ¼" smaller than the diameter of the button because the felt stretches.

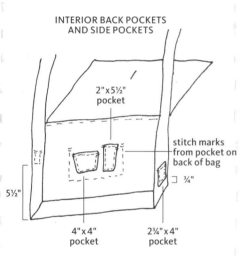

INTERIOR BACK POCKETS AND SIDE POCKETS

2" x 5½" pocket

stitch marks from pocket on back of bag

¾"

5½"

4" x 4" pocket

2¾" x 4" pocket

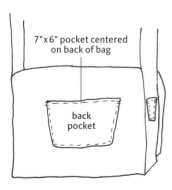

7" x 6" pocket centered on back of bag

back pocket

step 3

Tool Pocket

FINISHED DIMENSIONS
13¼" x 5"

MATERIALS

Red tool pocket:

13¼" x 14" red felt, for case

Oatmeal felt: Two ½" x 36" pieces (for straps) and 3" x 4½" (for needle holder)

Rose felt: 5½" x ½" (for needle holder strap) and 2" x 2½" (for inner pin holder)

Embroidery floss in red (for case construction) and white (for attaching straps and needle holder)

Gold tool pocket:

13¼" x 14" gold felt, for case

Rose felt: Two ½" x 36" pieces (for straps) and 3" x 4½" (for needle holder)

Mint green felt: 5½" x ½" (for needle holder strap) and 2" x 2½" (for inner pin holder)

Embroidery floss in grass green (for case construction) and brick red (for attaching straps and needle holder)

STITCHES USED

Whipstitch, Straight Stitch. Instructions for these stitches can be found on pages 14–15.

At the end of a long day of stitching, I always wrap up my tools—rulers, scissors, glue stick, thread, and needles—in my tool pocket. When I reopen the pocket the next morning, everything is there as I left it, ready for a new day of stitching. I fill my tool pocket with just what I need, relegating any extra items and doodads to more permanent, less portable locales.

1. Fold and Sew Case

   Following the drawing on page 112, fold the case felt to make a 5"-deep pocket (the folded piece of felt will measure 13¼" x 9") and pin the sides together. Using 3-ply embroidery floss, tie a knot on the inside bottom edge of one folded side. Whipstitch to close the edge, using stitches no more than ¼" apart. Knot off on the inside at the top edge of the pocket. Repeat on the other side.

   With single-ply floss, tie a knot on the inside edge at the top of the pocket (at the end of a line of whipstitches). Straight stitch across the open edge of the pocket, being careful to sew through that layer of felt only. Continue stitching around the perimeter of the flap and knot off on the inside when you reach the other top edge of the case.

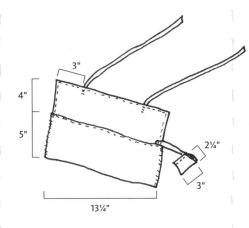

3"

4"

5"

2¼"

3"

13¼"

Steps 1 and 3

step 3

2. Attach Straps

With the flap closed, pin the straps onto the outside of the flap 3" from each side, allowing 1" of each strap to overlap the flap edge (see photograph opposite).

Using 6-ply floss, tie a knot on the wrong side of the flap under one strap and sew 5 straight stitches one on top of the other, parallel to the base of the case, to affix the full 1" of strap to the case felt. Knot off on the wrong side of the flap. Repeat for the other strap.

3. Create and Attach Needle Holder

Fold the needle holder felt in half, sandwiching the small piece of felt in between (creating a book cover with one page). Pin the felt pieces in place and, using 6-ply floss, tie a knot at one corner inside the book and hide the loose end. Straight stitch along the fold to form a "spine," removing pins as you sew. At the other edge, attach the book to the needle holder strap using 2 straight stitches. Knot off as you did the other knot. Sew 3 straight stitches, attaching the loose end of the needle holder strap to the inner upper right corner of the tool pocket. Knot off on the inside of the pocket.

To tie the straps around the closed tool pocket, see the photograph on page 110 and the drawing at left.

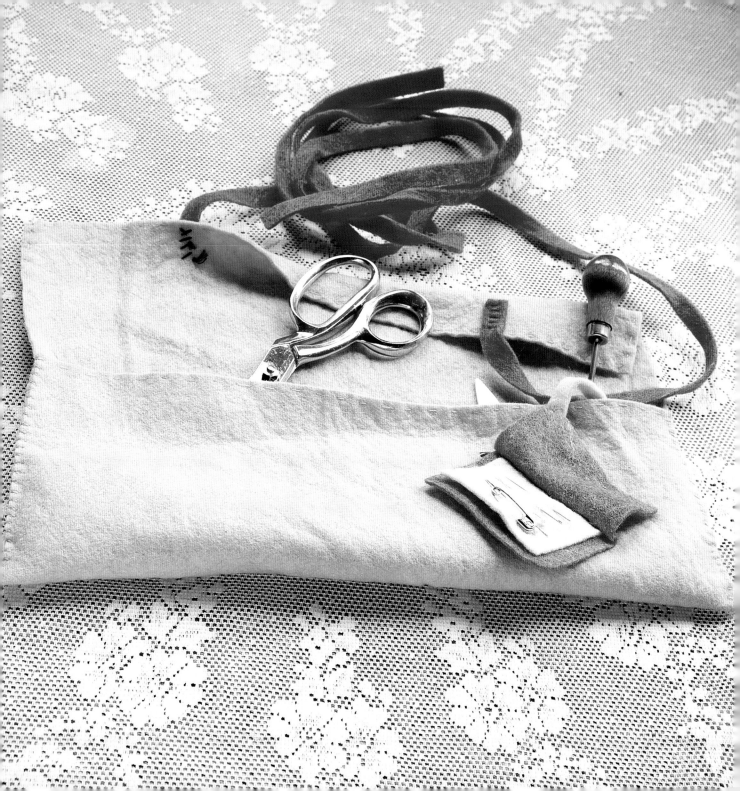

PART 3

Templates

Working with Templates

Most of the projects in this book require that you use a template to cut out a piece of felt. In order to do this, you will first need to photocopy the template at the percentage suggested in each project. (You could also mix and match templates to create a variety of appliqués, reducing or enlarging accordingly.) Next, cut out the template pieces from the photocopy with paper scissors and use the paper patterns as a guide for cutting out the felt pieces. Lay the paper templates on the felt, safety pin them in place, and cut around the edges with fabric shears. You can also transfer the design by tracing around the perimeter of the cut-out template onto felt with a fine-tipped permanent marker. Remove the paper template and cut out the shape just inside the lines.

abcde
fghijkl
mnopqr
stuvw
xyz

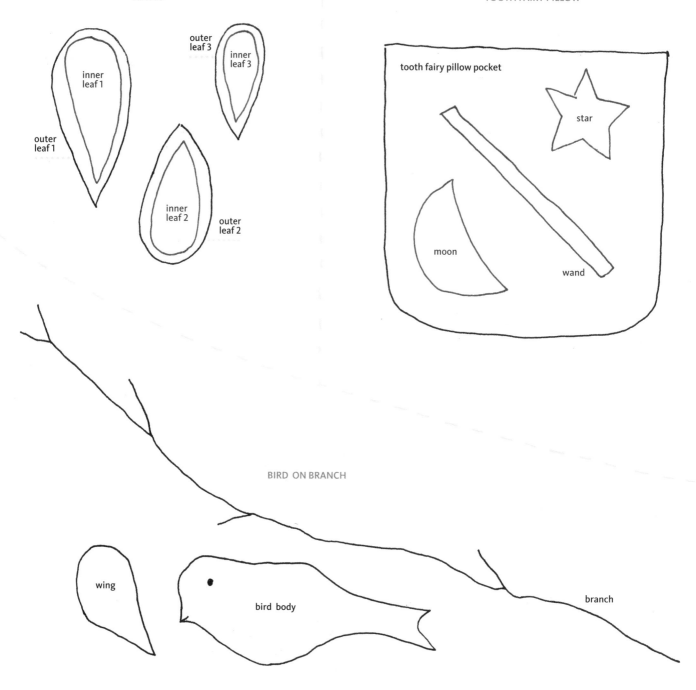

LEAVES

inner leaf 1

outer leaf 1

outer leaf 3

inner leaf 3

inner leaf 2

outer leaf 2

TOOTH FAIRY PILLOW

tooth fairy pillow pocket

star

moon

wand

BIRD ON BRANCH

wing

bird body

branch

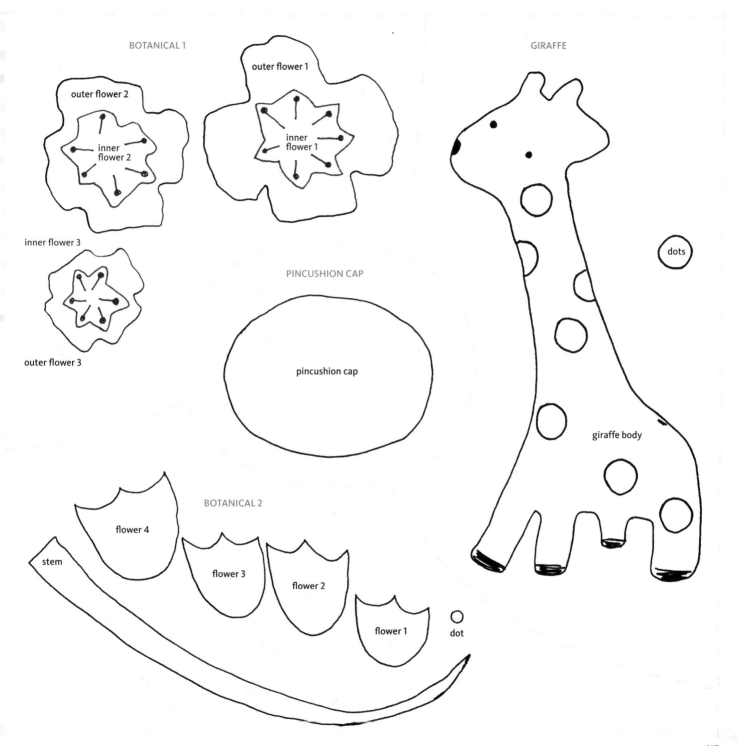

BOTANICAL 1

outer flower 2

inner flower 2

outer flower 1

inner flower 1

inner flower 3

outer flower 3

PINCUSHION CAP

pincushion cap

GIRAFFE

dots

giraffe body

BOTANICAL 2

flower 4

flower 3

flower 2

stem

flower 1

dot

DOG

dog ear

dog body

outer mouse puppet ear

inner mouse puppet ear

MOUSE FINGER PUPPET

mouse puppet body

snail shell

SNAIL

snail body

mouse puppet tail

ELEPHANT

skirt

shorts

shoe

hand

ear

sleeve

elephant head

jacket

RABBIT PATCH

rabbit head/arms

dress

overalls

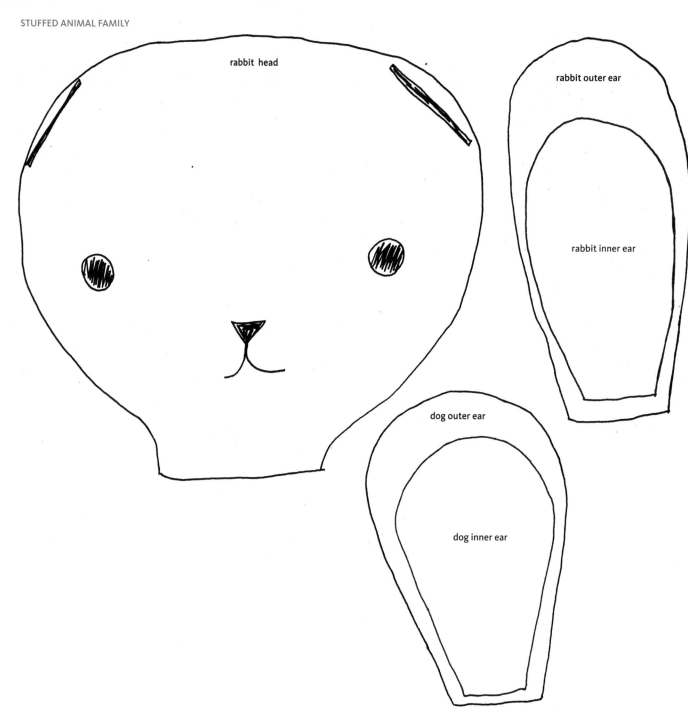

rabbit head

rabbit outer ear

rabbit inner ear

dog outer ear

dog inner ear

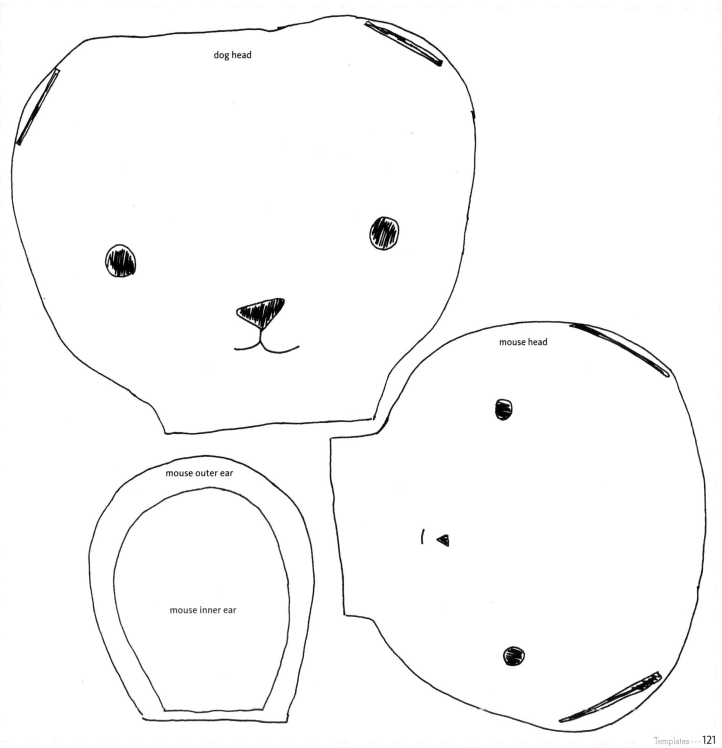

dog head

mouse head

mouse outer ear

mouse inner ear

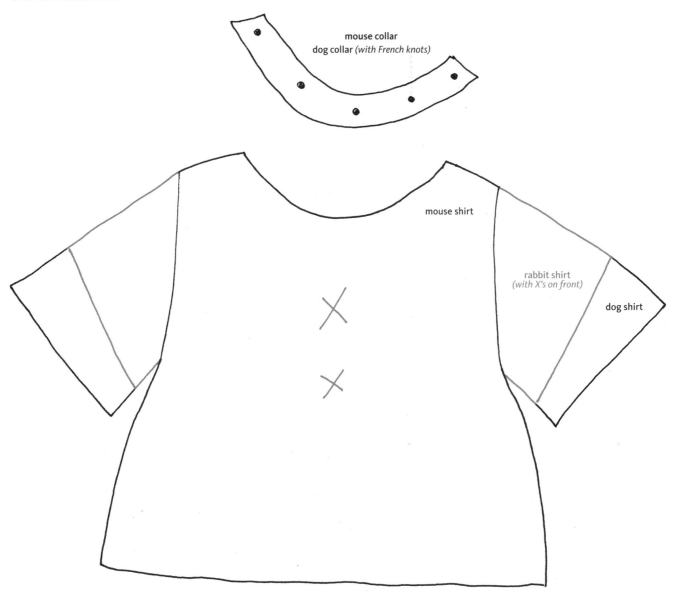

mouse collar
dog collar *(with French knots)*

mouse shirt

rabbit shirt
(with X's on front)

dog shirt

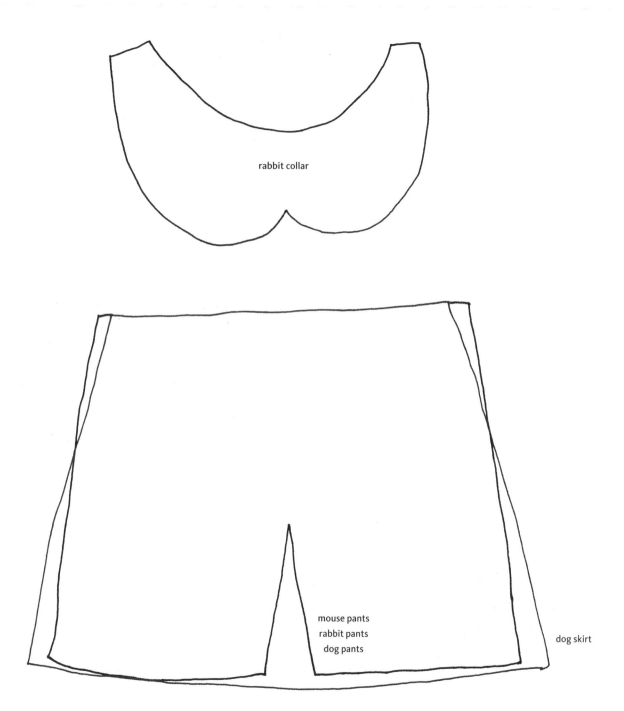

rabbit collar

mouse pants
rabbit pants
dog pants

dog skirt

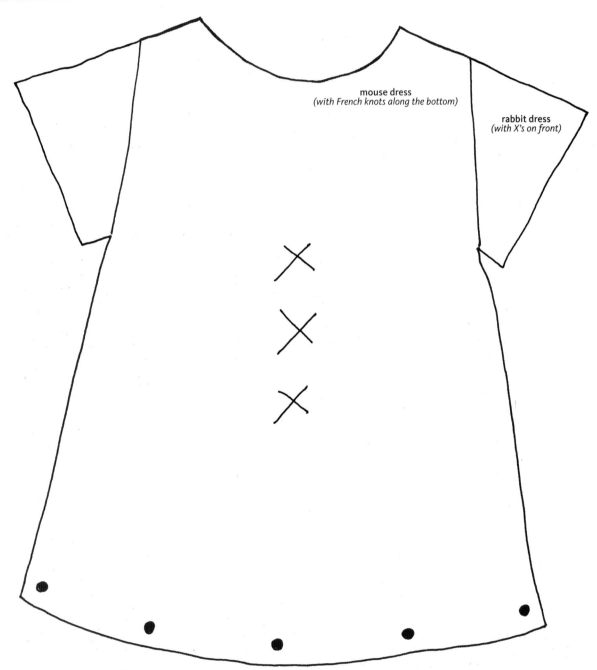

mouse dress
(with French knots along the bottom)

rabbit dress
(with X's on front)

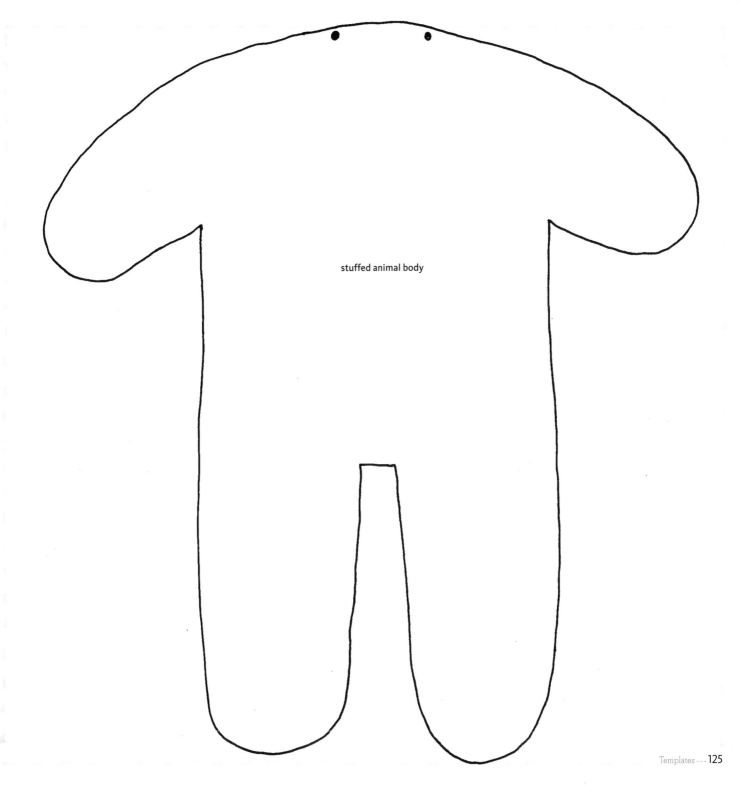

stuffed animal body

Resources

General Supplies

The materials and tools used in the projects in this book are generally available at fabric and craft stores nationwide. If you cannot find what you are looking for locally, try your favorite online sources or the ones listed here:

Jo-Ann Fabric and Craft
www.joann.com

Purl Patchwork
www.purlsoho.com

ReproDepot Fabrics
www.reprodepot.com

Sources for Felt

The felt used for the projects shown in this book is pure wool (or 70% wool/ 30% rayon), most of which is hand-dyed at Kata Golda. Our felt is available at www.katagolda.com or www.ohmafelt.com. At the Kata Golda web site you can also buy kits that contain precut felt and embroidery floss for each project in this book.

The pure wool hand-dyed felts from the companies listed below will also work well.

A Child's Dream Come True
www.achildsdream.com

Magic Cabin
www.magiccabin.com

Or, in a pinch, you can even repurpose fabric from felted wool sweaters.

Acknowledgments

On a whim one day I carefully wrapped up a copy of my catalog, stitched a personalized tag to the package, and sent it off to Melanie Falick at STC Craft. To my great surprise, I received a phone call a few weeks later from Liana Allday, an editor who works with Melanie, saying that they were interested in publishing my work! My many thanks for STC's enthusiasm for my project. Thank you, Liana, for your clarity, great care, and attention.

Thank you to Lana Lê of woolypear for understanding my vision and bringing it to life in your beautiful design.

Thank you to the beautiful people that appear in my book: Jaden, Linda, and Odette.

Thank you to my great helpers at Kata Golda: Akiko Chriss, Janet Goff, Beth O'Neal, Deb Oldham, Randelle Schmidt, and Kerry Shamblin.

Thank you Sid, Tony, Walt, Jen G., Jeb B., and Karen.

Thank you Palace Hotel and Vintage Hardware.

Thank you to Julie Cummings, my dear friend who helped me draw with scissors.

Thank you to Tracy Harding, who inspired the beginnings of my felt stitchery.

Thank you to Sorcha Ashling, who is the Kata Golda backbone.

Thank you to Amy Redmond, designer, letterpress printer, and hula hooper extraordinaire!

Thank you to my beautiful daughter, S. Odette Jennings, who reads to me and plays piano while I stitch, and who provides me with endless inspiration.

Thank you to my photographer, my best friend, and my soul mate, Frankie.